A Survivor's Guide to Building Your Own Home

Lez Gray

Waterways World Ltd
Burton on Trent

Published by Waterways World Ltd,
151 Station Street, Burton-on-Trent,
Staffordshire DE14 1BG, England

© Lez Gray 2003

This edition first published 2003

British Library Cataloguing In Publication Data
A catalogue record for this book is available from
the British Library

ISBN 1 870002 98 9

Cover design by Paul Limbert

Editing, design and layout by Sylvia Fallows

Printed and bound in the United Kingdom
by Page Bros, Norwich

ACKNOWLEDGEMENTS/DEDICATION

This tome is dedicated first and foremost with love and amazement to my co-conspirator, best friend and wife Mandy, whose curriculum vitae now includes mum, builders mate and self build co-dependent.
The second debt of thanks goes to Audrey, my mother, for shelter, support, storage space and sticky buns on demand.

Now to the support crew.
First up are Nick and Tina Mansfield-Ward for hot baths, 'Red Cross' food parcels and just being there when it rained (which was often).
To Graham and Barbara Field for sanctuary, support and buying the wine when we ran out of paint and money (in more ways than one).
To my old mate Andy Wilczur, sentenced over many weekends to hard labour and seeing the funny side of it all.
To Paul and Andrea Moon/Eversley for reminding us why, generally helping out and bringing gifts when it mattered.
An honourable mention also goes to Kim Sales of Jewson plc for changing my mind about salesmen.
The final thanks go to Ross Stokes, editor of *SelfBuild&Design* magazine for help in both giving this book life and in keeping lentils on my plate.

FOREWORD
by Ross Stokes, editor of *SelfBuild & Design*

Every year, an estimated 20,000 individual homes are built in the UK. These are known collectively as 'self builds'. For the uninitiated this can be a confusing description. After all, it implies that the owners have builttheir homes with their own hands. This is rarely the case. Often the selfbuilder limits his physical input to thumbing through books of house plans, and simply letting the builders get on with it. Only a select group of die-hards will take on the actual construction work themselves.

Most selfbuilders will want to get involved in some way though, usually to save money. Les Gray falls into this latter category. As an IT specialist, he started out knowing little about the building game but found himself on a sharp learning curve when he was forced to manage his build to save money.

And what began as a supporting role, ordering materials and employing contractors, gradually evolved into a more hands-on approach, with Les installing both the electrics and the plumbing, as well as the bespoke kitchen.

It wasn't all plain sailing, as he is the first to admit. There were some scary moments. But Les has emerged from it all mentally and physically unscathed – and with his dream home worth considerably more than it cost to build.

Indeed, Les enjoyed the experience so much he felt compelled to write this book to share his experiences – and tips – with others contemplating the same route. As an office worker with little more than a few basic DIYskills, he can empathise with those who find the prospect daunting. But he has demonstrated that it is possible for virtually anyone to complete their own self build – providing they are sensible.

This book is not designed to be a definitive guide to self build – there are already several excellent books on the market. Rather, it is an honest and humorous account of one particular self build. An experience which has clearly changed the author's life forever.

By reading this book it could change your life too.

CONTENTS

Chapter 1

Introduction

You're reading this book. Good. My guess is that you have toyed with the idea of building your own home for a while, and boy isn't there a lot of stuff out there vying for your trade and commitment? Perhaps you have already been to one or more self build shows? Maybe the current media coverage on renovation and DIY has fired you up enough to buy a magazine on the subject. Fear not, I'm in there, too, somewhere between *Waterways World* and *Ideal Home* magazine. You see I was once like you: looking, wondering, thinking about it.

Then one day I got up enough momentum to actually go through with it. When I started there were probably about three decent books on the subject. The first by the patron saint of selfbuilders, Murray Armour, the second by Rosalind Renshaw, and the third, a sort of materials listing manual, by Mark Brinkley. Each had their own merits, but since I wanted to build a timber frame and do most of the work myself, they only gave me a part of the story.

You see, I am one of those restless types who believes that with enough time and resources all things are within reach. I was wrong and I was right in varying proportions.

So, dear reader, this book is for you. It is the story of someone who started with enough nous to wire a 13 amp plug, but ended up designing and installing all of it. It is about the upstart who dared to ask the secret brotherhood of plumbers for their most sacred knowledge before doing all manner of things with boilers and underfloor heating.

And finally it's about the fervent DIYer who reached beyond his grasp and fell on numerous occasions on his backside. Sometimes smiling, sometimes whining. But always learning. There is another part of this story to give a balance to things. Let's call it the wife's tale. If you are married or partnered in any way and you are contemplating this thing they romantically call self build, then it's not just the house project which will undergo change.

Chapter two will just give you a flavour of what we went through before the fun really started, whilst Chapter 8 offers up some survival aids.

Another real eye opener along the way was the assortment of characters we met and employed. Their candour and openness frequently amazed, often irritated, but seldom bored us. Many laid open their private lives for all to see. All the time I kept a diary.

So I make no pretensions of being any sort of expert. Simply put, I – sorry we – did it. Warts and all! Ours is the 1500sq.ft timber frame bungalow sitting half way up a village hill trying to blend in with the trees.

Nothing went smoothly with even the company that supplied the frame going bust two months after we took delivery. Which was close. Looking back, we did it the hard way and learned many hard lessons along the way. These I offer to you. Yes, I do hope to sell enough of this tome to pay for a well earned holiday. But mostly this is for those stubborn types with whom I wholly identify who think that they might just like to have a go. We did eighty per cent of the work ourselves.

This ranged from helping manhandle the block and beam floor into place, to laying the foundation for the fireplace. We left anything structural and subject to warranties well alone. Thus leaving electrics, plumbing, carpentry (including building the kitchen from scratch) and anything else that needed doing.

Overall project management was also down to me and perhaps the first lesson to learn is the difficulty in trying to be boss and tradesman at the same time. Looking back, I am sure we could have broken less of those spinning plates had I stuck to simply one thing.

However, new skills were learned and I ruthlessly probed the trade for answers when I did not know any better. Mostly they answered with good grace and charity. Sometimes they slammed the doors in my face. But never forget: building your own home no matter what level of hands-on you opt for is not for the faint-hearted. Your friends will either think you are nuts or they will admire you. Ageing parents, likewise. In fact, this beast affects most everyone with whom you come in contact. The wheat is certainly sorted from the chaff in this little exercise. Our better friends threw us lifelines and unconditional hot baths when needed. The others perhaps got lost in the Christmas card lists.

In writing this book it is my belief that too many publications dwell on the financial rewards of simply cutting out the speculative builder for a straight cash reward. That's fine if making a fast buck is all you need from the project. However, it is my experience that most selfbuilders do so to get the home of their dreams and at a price they might not of otherwise afforded.

This was certainly the case with our home. In fact, one visitor described the project as a manifesto. Which, I think, was flattering ? I do believe, however, that as rewarding as it is, these publications only give half the story. Even wealthy folk who pay someone to do all the work for them find this a stressful and physically demanding pastime.

So in writing this book it was my aim to lay bare the experiences and lessons we picked up. To tell it as it happened. Our approach tended to the extreme in hands-on so I am well placed to both encourage and educate, hopefully in equal measure. The tone of the book I hope is chatty and not overburdened with building jargon. However, in some places this is inevitable and here I offer a glossary of jargon as an appendix.

I realise (though you might not yet) how busy you are going to be, so I have summarised the lessons learned from the main stages at the end of each appropriate section, for those of you too busy to read all the narrative.

So would we do it again ? Right now, definitely not. It's now three years since we started this campaign and we are exhausted and just want to enjoy what we've achieved so far. The future? Maybe, but differently. Perhaps I'll re-read this book and remember some of the tips and go for it again. Or maybe I'll just be content that some of you had a go for yourselves. Enjoy.

Chapter 2

Odes of mud and estate agents

It is March 1998. We are about as far from Cambridge as a crow on steroids could get without falling over the edge of the postcode, and our stake is in this piece of sod. There are two lines of trees and ten seasons of unmoved wilderness. To the front, an old rusty gate and three miles of bramble. It is boggy underfoot and the stinking boulder clay, which has just added several zeros to the foundation costs, sucks at your wellies as you walk. But to me it is beautiful. Only someone with the dewy eyed optimism of a selfbuilder could see its potential. That someone was us. Some other prospects had already stuck their heads over the fence and asked questions. To these we bared our teeth and made sandwiches. They did not return.

So this is journey's end. Many moons have passed with as many miles and manky plots viewed the length and breadth of southern England. Previously we had ventured west to Devon and Cornwall. Here we broke bread with the commune dwellers and dreamers we found there. Alas, dreams and ideals neither pay mortgages nor put bread on the table. We also learned quickly that barn conversions go cheap in south western parts. Cheap, that is, until the planners get hold of the materials list and insist that the pixies hand carve the local stones for your brickwork. Or that only antique reclaimed widgets can be used to hold the walls up! The other big truth about dream plots in Utopia is that they are cheap for a reason. No bugger can get work to pay the mortgage! So we started doing the National Lottery and drifted ever northwards. Then one night, gathered around the campfire, an old timer spoke of a place where self build plots as big as your

5

overdraft were there for the asking. The locals were friendly, and the planners as helpful as could be to folks like us. But no amount of gold could persuade us to live in Milton Keynes. However, the compass was set and we began to look more seriously at the northern home counties. Firstly onto the semi-industrial flatlands of Northants where for about fifty grand you could build your very own nuclear power plant from the local ironstone.

Then onto the Fenlands of north Cambridgeshire. Very handy for Cambridge they told us. Very handy if you are a mallard or marsh harrier that is. All the while with character and potential thrown in. One plot we skipped through very quickly offered a constant source of cheap diesel from the industrial estate next door. Trust me, if you think describing existing real estate is a tad on the creative side, you ain't seen nothing till you let an estate agent describe a blank building plot.

In total we spent something like twelve months living with friends and doing the bed and breakfast trail like some demented RAC/Lombard rally across our nation. Now we are here. Discretely tucked away in the Cambridgeshire-Bedfordshire borderlands, cosseted by the M11 to our right, the A1 to the left and the A14 up above. The estate agents like this village a lot, and we have about one third of an acre of it.

So why not just buy a home off the shelf like most normal folk ? Ah, you see it is that word *normal* that gives it away. Normal by mathematical definition is a sort of average, a mid point in a graph of behaviour types. Talking to folk who self build will reveal a most definite non average run-with-the-pack mentality. Okay, we are odd, we crave the individuality of not just designing but actually putting something of ourselves into our homes.

Perhaps it was the opportunity to plan the exact size and shape of the living space to our needs, as opposed to those of a bulk build developer. Or maybe the assurance of high quality materials and construction beyond the norm. Either way, it is unique and it cost less than we could otherwise have afforded. It also stretched our relationship to the edge and back, leaving us wondering where all the money and time went. And those were the good points.

The real beginning for us goes back to somewhere in the mid 1980s and a chance encounter with a Potton Homes glossy. A work colleague of mine had been leering at great length at all the things he could do for about a quarter of the price. Mansions abounded, so I prised the subversive material from his sweaty palms and made a phone call. It did not end there. Once the barbs were in it took another decade to work its dark way inwards, and by the early 90s we were regulars at the infamous Alexandra Palace Self Build shows.

Next came the brochures and selling of the souls to land agencies and anyone who could spell building plot. About this time media interest and a host of so-called experts began popping up everywhere. Self build is a drug and we both had a problem. Fixes came in short bursts. Chance meetings with people that had done it before. Some several times. These we called gods and reverently their brains we picked. We drawled over pictures of Swedish log cabins and mock Tudor farmhouses. But all the while the cravings grew. Something had to give. Time for brass tacks and the cold slap of reality every wannabe self builder has to pass through. How much? What ? Where ? Do we have enough to do it? That particular time we did not, we could not. For the first time builder having a sizeable wedge up front is a pre-requisite. Looking at it from the money lender's point of view I can see why. We had neither experience of construction nor trade skills. Not even expertise in a related discipline such as surveying etc. Even though we both earned a good living it was just too risky for the pinstripe fundholders. However, it was and remains time well spent. We regrouped, re-assessed our position and kept our eyes on the horizon to see what the tide would bring in. We did not have to wait long.

Now it is May 1995 and somewhere in amongst the classified section of the only self build magazine then on the market, we chanced upon what was a probably the first self build brokerage company. Mandy (the missus) made the first of many phone calls to a bloke with a surname with far too many Zs and Cs in it. A deal was spoken of involving a small syndicate of wannabes like us somewhere in the posher parts of Essex. The return on investment potential was there up front and in bright letters. Very Des Res in the right part of town. Mandy said yes, I hesitated and said no. The short Polish bloke who wanted to be rich said he would come and spell it all out for us. We were the last (it turned out) to sign up. Time was running out and he needed us to close the deal. In retrospect I'm glad he did. So five of us contracted a NHBC builder to construct five brick and block detached homes in the pleasant Essex countryside.

From the very start, nothing went smoothly. Firstly, our home was built a couple of metres too near to our neighbour's house. The whole thing became (between clenched teeth) a laughable cock up and collectively we put the builder out of business for malpractice. But the development from a financial point of view was everything and more.

Once the plastering had stopped falling onto our friends' children (whilst bathing) it allowed us to do what we wanted to do all along. Build our own, properly. So many lessons learned along the way. From adversity much wisdom.

Now it is 1997 and I am touting my wares as a professional project manager working in the computing game. With a healthy wedge in the bank and about 12 months of research behind us we are ready to go shopping. However, the words simple and straightforward are not two adjectives that have ever sat comfortably together in our lives. You know those top ten most stressful things you can do to yourself? We went for it big time. Let's see. Move home, move in with in-laws, have couple of disastrous attempts at starting a family.

Then the really big one – pack in a 15 year career before you have a nervous breakdown and try to finance the whole thing for about a third of the previous income. If stress attracted air miles we could have gone around the world twice with enough to spare for a toaster! Just to put the final nail in the coffin we produced our first (and trust me our last) offspring about three quarters of the way into the build.

So to where it starts. It's muddy like only self build mud can be and there is a barely adequate ten foot ancient (and I mean ancient) touring caravan squeezed into the corner of the field.

We are still smiling because we have neither the sense nor the experience to know any different. More telling we are still waiting to get detailed planning permission.

Chapter 3

The plot, the planners and something else beginning with P (patience?)

There's a loop we all get (have been) stuck in. Where do we start? A design? Well yes, maybe? But until you have the plot and the planner's brief it is difficult to go very far down that route. What about money? Again yes, but at the beginning you only have some vague suggestions regarding on what figures you should base your budget. Potential financiers will want to see specifics which, of course, you don't have until you know how much they will give you. So it goes on. The added complication is that some financiers will also want some form of planning permission in evidence, sometimes outline but increasingly it's detailed. All of which means that you will have to speculate some of your own hard cash before parting someone else from theirs. I attacked the problem in parallel with actions on both the planning permission (we already had OPP) and finance fronts. Forecast budgeting started way back in time (more of which later). However, to stand any chance of breaking the loop you have to put a stake in the ground somewhere. Preferably not through the heart of the Chief Planning Officer (though it's tempting)So it is June 1997 and the invitation to tender for supplying a timber frame is down to a two house race. Time therefore to put some draft proposals together to see how the land lies with the planners. Chris (Medina Gimson, the eventual timber frame suppliers) and I are huddled over a planning brief to rival the Magna Carta. Which was bad enough. Unfortunately, there's more from a different quarter. The builder from whom we bought the land had originally intended to live next door with his aged parent. Mr Y has a habit of calling everyone by their surnames like taking a roll call. I suspect he is ex-Army and from the restrictive covenants he has left us must be one of Satan's own. Thankfully, he didn't move in but his legacy remained despite my best endeavours. "Thou shalt not keep pigs nor cockerels," says Chris. "What about geese or emus?" I ask trying to sound sincere. "No that's okay", says Chris trying not to choke on his beer. "Anything in there about orgies or wife swapping?" "No but here's something about washing your vegetables." I make a mental note never to wash my onions in an open drain, just in case. We are trying hard but without something tangible for the planners to criticise we realise our limitations and decide to go ahead with our best effort.

In the beginning Mandy and I had dreams of split level Scandinavian chalet style abodes. Our philosophy was (and remains) one of eco-friendly living long before the word became worn out on trendy peak time viewing. Early thoughts on design were as much shaped by what we had not liked in previous homes, as by what we thought we would like to see in a designed from scratch home. Lots of garden space was one ideal and this plot has it in bucket loads. We also have the real privilege of having a complete south facing garden with a pretty much uninterrupted skyline from dawn to dusk. With a potential expanse of roof the size of Northampton we are perfectly placed for loads of freebie solar energy. All that's required is consent to build the bungalow widthways incorporating the garage space within the main body of the dwelling.

As cold mortals, keeping warm was also high on our list so timber frame became a front runner early on as did underfloor heating. We wanted so much energy efficiency that just rolling over in bed would probably power the fridge for a week. Internally, every window space was to be stretched to a maximum size to keep the rooms bright and cheerful together with (effectively) triple glazing to trap all that solar heat. Mindful that most people think of bungalows as prefab chalets where one goes to retire we shamelessly pinched from another shed builder the idea of high vaulted ceilings in one half of the house. This, coupled with eccentric angles to add interest, would achieve acoustics to rival the Albert Hall!

Probably the main advantage of designing your own home from scratch is to design the living space around your own particular lifestyle. As trainee hedonists we like to cook, drink and entertain. So big open spaces for the kitchen/diner and an airing cupboard which doubles as a boiler room cum distillery is a must. Finally I make a mental note about the likely position of solar panels for the future. Naively, as it happens.

All sounds good doesn't it? Think again. In this game the planners always hold most of the cards. Having read repeatedly of the wisdom of checking things out with planners we tried at least to do things by the book (theirs not ours). So just days before contracts were to be exchanged we met on site with the planning department's tea boy. Of course we did not know at the time just how lowly a bod they had sent us but perhaps the Kit Kat in his overalls should have warned us. Anxious to please he is nodding approvingly at our tentative plans. It sounds okay and we are invited to go ahead with the application. Fortunately for us we have agreed a fixed price with the timber frame company to submit drawings and obtain detailed planning permission, no matter how many alterations, a smart move as it turns out. This particular plan means that some trees can be saved and we can have three rooms opening onto the garden. Romantic bliss. Chris, the salesman from Medina Gimson, scurries off – the ink still wet on his first cheque.

I believe that the term status quo was probably invented by a planner anxious not to allow too much adventurous spirit ruin a "let's all look the same way" mentality. Six weeks on they have rejected the proposal and rejected it big time. The integral garage is out, the house needs to be moved further back into the plot and the aspect turned through 90 degrees. Are they having a laugh? The two plots next door, on the other hand, have to go forward giving a kind of dog leg look to the building line. I begin to suspect that our boy planner is either on drugs or perhaps is too small a wheel in the machine.

Time and experience prove me correct on the latter. Here then is the lesson. Check out the credentials of whoever turns up on site and whether they have the clout to make even casual approvals. If in doubt ask to see the head of planning! Or at least get the head of the one that messed you about.

By comparison the final council's demands are a bit more on the planet. Brick samples and a landscaping plan are required before any work commences. I resist the mischief of suggesting wall to wall Leylandii Cyprus trees, the very sound of which conjures up images of rampaging triffids. But by this time we are on our knees and keen to comply. The Holy Grail is but a subclause away. It's late November 1997 and after much gritting of teeth and almost six months delay we obtain detailed planning permission.

Comparatively speaking, the production of the Building Regulation documents is a good deal less stressful. This then is the blue print of how the project is put together. The actual details of the document read like something out of a legal writ. But it is a language that the construction industry warms to and comprehends. Which is always good news. Getting quotations now is a good

13

deal easier and I must have run up hundreds of pounds in photocopying for every wannabe subcontractor who tendered for my business.

I recommend getting the architect to run off as many copies of the actual drawings as possible for two reasons: firstly they have access to Rambo-sized photocopying machines, and secondly because they always seem to drive new Volvos and therefore have too much money anyway!

To the sound of groundworkers sharpening their pencils it's time to bottom out the budget and formalise funding.

One of the first lessons I learned early on in my career concerns forecast budgeting. In total I must have spent 18 months trying to guesstimate how much the project would cost. Unfortunately the simple truth is that until you have the blueprint and drawings in your possession it is mostly educated guesswork. Take groundworks, for example. My quotes varied from £13,000 from one bloke in Reading to £1,700 from a local JCB one man band and his dog. One enterprising outfit at the 98 Self Build show even offered to come down from Newcastle because their soft southern equivalents were making bucket loads of dosh and didn't know how good they had it. The other problem concerns the degree of information you can actually give a potential quottee. Foundations are notoriously hard to determine until you start scraping away at the ground but by then it's too late. To minimise the risk I did three things. First I initiated dialogues with a couple of sympathetic building societies. Next I created a theoretical prototype of what we'd like if everything went our way (which of course it didn't). Finally, I commissioned a soil survey (and later on a foundation design).

Making contact with sympathetic ears takes a little time but eventually I narrowed it down to the Bradford and Bingley and the Nationwide. With both sides having nothing to lose I had a number of frank and extremely useful conversations before the size and location of the plot was even known. By the time we went cap in hand I knew the likely maximum loan against value, likely repayment costs and just how far they are likely to go in financing the dream together with what happens next if we decide to proceed.

I had a prototype running for at least a year even before planning permission was applied for, adding detail as it became available. Certainly the first detail concerned a notion of what sort of size measured in square feet (only planners seem to work in metric) we wanted as a minimum and the only way we could visualise what X amount of square footage looked like was by getting out the details of all the homes we had lived in previously. From this we had compiled a minimum list of requirements and came up with the figure of 1300sq.ft with a minimum of three bedrooms. As it turned out we have a 1500sq.ft bungalow with four bedrooms. The main point is that once we had compiled a theoretical project budget around a particular size of dwelling we had most of the information we needed to up or downsize our dream home, according to what the figures revealed. Anyway, I calculated the worst case scenario and added a bit.

Thankfully, some aspects of the build were a little easier to estimate. So many bricks equals so much coverage allowing, of course, for waste and breakage. Likewise, with roof tiles, plasterboard etc. The overall maxim for determining a budget is research. However, I quickly realised that I could never know as much about the build game or any subcontracted part of it as those who spend their time doing it over and over again. Try as we could there was never any way that we could foresee the hundreds of little bits of wood, plastic sheeting and felt battens that would be needed and the only way to offset ignorance is to keep a dialogue going with the tradesman (or woman) and try to identify what might be needed in addition to what you know (and, of course, persistent questioning). I found the quantity takeoffs that some builders merchants (such as Gibbs & Dandy) produce very helpful. Some of the big boys such as the roofing and piping companies (e.g. Marley Tile, OSMA etc) were especially helpful. Once again the golden Building Regs drawings were the key. Manufacturers had in 1998 woken up to the idea of self build and begun to operate a pretty in depth design service. I was then able to forward these to a couple of builders merchants for comparative costings.

At some point we had to put a stake in the ground and simply go for it. So how much contingency should you allow? Tales of selfbuilders running out of money are many, and whilst some tradespeople will smirk at your audacity for presuming to enter their world, most won't since nobody wins in the end. The man who laid my drive liked to sagely rub his chin, mutter something about my original groundworkers doing half a job then suggesting adding about £10,000 to the contingency fund. Which is nice if you are flush. The reality for us was that £10,000 would have meant not even starting. You do need some breathing space in there, though. In my budgeting I allowed 10% over net build budget and the mindset to delay or downsize our expectations regarding later cosmetics such as posh toilets etc.

Surprisingly, this is where a lot of the money can go. Many selfbuilders get to the last hurdle having accounted for every last masonry nail only to blow the budget on a posh loo at the finish. We focused on the core dwelling with all the necessary bits such as hot water and a cheap bath from B&Q. Self building if nothing else teaches you humility!

A strange thing happened when the words self build escaped from my lips the first time. Many financial bods blanched over and suggested opening up a vein. Then there were the more enlightened types. Perhaps they have watched something on the box and heard enough return on investment figures to start them salivating. Mike at the Nationwide was one such man. He's young, slick and on the ball. But most of all he knows a good business proposal when it makes an appointment. We had spoken on and off for over six months and chewed over the figures. Now I am here in person with my spreadsheet and a mission to build. We chat for about half an hour and it quickly appears we have more at stake than they do so a few formalities pass, palms are pressed and the money is ours. Most of the advance will be up front which is really good news. Firstly because it can go into a high interest cheque account when it's not paying bills (the interest from which will keep fish and chips on our plates when we cannot be bothered to lift a finger to cook, which is Fridays, usually). And secondly because my haggle power with suppliers just went ballistic due to the fact I could pay them promptly.

Many others would not entertain our case in particular because my wife carried the flag and the family funding on her shoulders. However, whilst the salaries stacked up something strange, even in the late 20th century, was happening again and again. I call it "sprogophobia". This is the phenomenon (please resist singing that Muppet song) of reluctance to advance a mortgage against a woman's salary just in case she gets pregnant. Thinking about it I wonder why there aren't many women building society managers out there. Perhaps they are scared that they will give all the money away to broody investors. The irony was that we did have a sprog about half way through the build. And stranger still it was me that stayed at home changing nappies with one hand and fitting bathroom tiles with the other.
Strange times indeed! New man stays at home and builds house, who'da thought it? Anyway, to assurances of my ultimate return to conventional employment we secured funding.

So now all the bits were in place. I turned off the computer, reached for my wellies and headed out for the proper business of the day. I need a soil engineer, a groundworker and, most importantly, a portable toilet.

Chapter 4

Breaking sod, or groundworks and services

Before the days of Bridget Jones, a scruffy almost middle-aged bloke wearing combat trousers and a bobble hat with a rude slogan upon his brow, moved his modest possessions and tired old carcass onto a building site.

No electricity nor basic comforts did he have for they were truly in the pipeline. And this was good.

Thereupon he commenced to keep his own diary of the events to come upon an aged laptop computer running on old batteries.

The words that follow are less Adrian Mole more Bob the Builder meets James Herriot in an opium den in the local builders merchants (for some times things were mighty peculiar)I originally toyed with the notion of editing these diary entries into a coherent dialogue about the early days but having reread them a few times I think the spirit of the times are best presented raw as they happened.

Monday 16th March 1998

This is the advance party. The pre-emptive strike if you like. I have a 10 foot caravan circa 1978 and a free standing water pipe. That's it, folks, the height of luxury. It took three strong men a high mileage Vauxhall Cavalier and a lot of high quality cursing to tuck her next to the hedge out of the way of marauding Travellers and delivery drivers. But this is it, my home for more months than we ever dreaded. Fortunately, it's early spring and things might just get better. For the moment I am on my own until Mandy works her notice and moves in with me. This makes us feel like we're dating again with nightly visits to the local phone box with all the news.

The soil engineers have left me two very deep survey holes within tripping distance (in the dark) of the caravan and I consider whether to place flashing lights around them to avoid trapping erring hedgehogs. They (the soil people) also told me what I already thought I knew: that a glacier passed this way, oh about 2 million years ago. Now it's official and the appropriate type of foundation can be designed. Better still is the implicit liability if they are wrong. The holes begin to fill up below the spring line and the question of how to keep clean becomes clear to me. It's early days and the novelty of enforced bachelor life keeps me amused. I cannot help but wonder how the missus will cope in such Spartan conditions. Then I remember that she has survived two Glastonburys and living with my mother, no worries. After all, self build women are as tough as old boots. But they do like to bathe more than once a month. Must remember to check out the local swimming pool. I can almost see the faces of the reception staff as two muddy Herberts turn up every other night for a scrub down and a cup of vending machine tea. It will probably explain in time why the filters keep on blocking up. You see it's that glacier's fault!

Then the day finally arrived. The day when all those hardened cynics will be put firmly to shame. A JCB, a dump truck and his mate called Ron turned up at 0730 hours with but one aim in life: "to get it out the ground and filled quick as you like". There I stood like a newly acquired acolyte watching in awe as the men that do, did. What wonders are performed with a piece of string, a spray can of yellow chalk and some miraculous device called a Theodolite. Before I could say dpc we had a giant hopscotch table neatly lined out on the previously virgin sod. Must be time for a cuppa, I reasoned, and I know you lads all have two sugars. But no, shock horror, not a single grain of Tate and Lyle's finest. Must be new men, I thought, probably only eat wholemeal bread too. I tried reason, it says so in all the books, said I. "Well," says Ron, who's a dead ringer for Bob Hoskins, "If we're doing it by the bleedin' book I'm going home. You see the trouble wiv these soddin' books is the same wiv them old barstewards what sit in offices designing foundations fer owses, yer see until you get yer arse wet on site an you can see wot roots yer actually got, it don't mean nuffin 'nless you can see it yerself".

I feel admonished and return to make the tea sans sucre. It's several hours on and the A-team are looking perplexed. As honouree project manager (and ultimately he wot pays em) I'm invited over to peer into a hole for a decision. "Wot pillock'd do that ?" says Sandy (to JCBs what Damon Hill is to rally driving). We're looking at the remains of someone's soakaway absolutely bang smack in the middle of my footings trench. We look at the colour of the bricks in the offending hole we look at each other we look again.   "That bird from building control ain't gonna like that," they say. Time for an executive decision. "Rip it out," say I, with an authority borrowed from Star Trek's Captain Jean Luc Picard (therefore even when you're not sure, sound like you know what you're talking about with conviction and a RSC delivery if possible). We proceed various people from the utilities turn up with something called conduit (which I thought was posh for salt and pepper) for me to lay in the trench (with a hockey stick at each end apparently, and "don't forget to tie the pull through string at the ends with a block of wood"). Then the highlight of the day. There we are merrily building a spoil heap to rival open cast mining on the neighbouring plot for which I have previously gained permission (temporarily, until the muck away lorry arrives). There I am happily collecting broken bricks with which to prop up the steel mesh in my foundations (whilst they pour the cement in). Arrival stage left, like something from the Flying Squad, of my new neighbour's father, would you believe ? It transpires that unbeknown to yours truly contracts are about to be exchanged on the plot next door. I'm wearing combat trousers and a hat that says "same shit another day" and I haven't shaved for two days. "Whose in charge?" says DI Reagan. "I am," say I. Some words are exchanged during which the dreadful truth dawns. Yes, this scruffy Herbet owns the bloody land and will be neighbour in residence to both his beloved siblings (two plots you see, its like having the Waltons move in next door, where Grandpa packs an Uzi). We shake hands words are unsaid. Guffaws all round. I make a mental note not to borrow any cups of sugar. Time to heat up my pasta, open a solitary can of grog and dream of when the missus moves in.

Tuesday 17th March 1998

A woman on a horse turned up today. "Oi delivers the mail," says she from on high. Turns out she's the village postie. I wonder where she kept the sacks. We get onto village life and the influx of them outlanders, surely she can't mean me! "You see I'm a village person" she says. I resist doing the YMCA dance. I figure it's best not to incense the locals too much at this early stage, especially as the dynamic duo have just turned up and they are scary enough in their own right. I've also learned my first lesson of the cosmic world of building. If your groundie says eight o'clock in the morning that really means seven. Early enough to catch the boss in his caravan asleep and ready for the dulcet tones of a JCB exhaust in his left ear. I learn early on that this game of how early shall we start progresses down the line with the hours getting later with subsequent subbies. "Sod 'em," I think, nothing comes between the serious selfbuilder and his constitutional muesli and cuppa at seven o'clock.

We are into the remainder of the footings today when we hit a conflict of interest. The brickie wants the concrete to finish at one level to keep his coursing (brick layers to you and me) right. Ron, who happens to have done everything including bricklaying, has his own definite view on the matter. "You tell 'im to get 'is rod an level down here," he says between gritted teeth.

This was the beginning of what was to be a long hate-hate relationship with neither of the parties ever meeting. I learn early on that every trade seems intent on knocking every other trade on site. We remonstrate and the logic of the man on site (being nine tenths of the argument) wins the day. I am allowed to make my first decision of the day. "Make it so," say I. After all, if the crew of Star Trek ever built a house that's what Captain Picard would say. Maybe Ron was a Klingon warrior in a previous life, all that pent up aggression, perhaps I'll suggest meditation to him!

The second decision is but a JCB scoop away. I always know when trouble beckons because it starts with Ron and Sandy hunched over the setting out drawings. "Who did yer take-off fer the metalwork?" they say. I look guilty. "Well I did with the help of the builders merchants, why?" Seems I have under estimated the steel mesh. My penance is twofold.

Firstly, I am dispatched for more metalwork. Secondly, I am allowed to cut the existing mesh into trench sized lengths with a pair of blunt bolt croppers. Now this a task designed to weed out the greenhorns from the groundworkers (who are well 'ard, with an "A"). By the end of this phase I have a new set of muscles, a squint and a strange new way of walking.

Breaking sod, or groundworks and services

Later that morning I get to meet the local building control officer. Mindful of their fearsome reputation and potential to seriously upset the self build can of worms I have mixed emotions about this inaugural visit. But I need not have worried as a very attractive young lady and her boss in tow turn up late morning just as I'm co-ordinating the delivery of the site Portaloo. The culmination of these two events leaves Ron in a spin. "Cor" he says "we don't normally get kazzis till after the brickies have been in". Between lust and the prospect of posh ablutions things just keep getting better for my boys. I top off the morning with chocolate Hobnobs (biscuits), clearly I'm spoiling them. Said young lady skips briefly around the maze that is our new home's foundations and nods conspiratorially to the groundies. Next they speak in some foreign tongue about mesh and slump and away she goes. Apparently we have passed. I am convinced that I have witnessed an ancient ritual with members of a secret fraternity. They all know their roles, things go smoothly and I am content.

Ron has a philosophy on most things. This one involves footwear. "Anyone what wears rigger boots and carries a clipboard is either a site manager, inspector or general management plonker". Then one turns up in a pristine four wheel drive and pink complexion. Ron takes the audience's appreciation. The rigger boot wearer does exactly the same as building control but this time on behalf of the insurance company underwriting the build. Without the ritual he smiles and departs, rigger boots none the worse for the experience. As we huddle over lunch in anticipation of a convoy of concrete trucks the last of officialdom's best turns up from the building society's valuation department. Clearly they've saved the best till last as this one not only has rigger boots but packs a rifle in his spare time. Do we want anything shot? he asks. Vermin, foxes, rats? Well the rats come later in the story but the family bunny took one look, stamped the ground to warn his mates in the wild and buried himself in the hutch. I decline to comment in the best interest of securing the building society's dosh.

One of the real eye openers of this build I discover early on is the willingness of people to open up about their lives. This invariably goes beyond the run of the mill stuff. Within the first few weeks of the build I discovered a whole new dimension to what we blokes call playing away from home.

No names shall I relate here but suffice to say that the network extends way beyond the construction game touching on one bloke's accountant's wife, two football groupies, a gaggle of dryliners and at least one plumber's mate. All of the above prompted by speculation over one young lady's lips earlier that morning.

Before we get too carried away the additional steelwork for the foundation turns up on the back of a juggernaut. The driver seems to come from the wilds of Scotland and I only understand every third word of what he's trying to tell me.

"An'll whey doon ta A1 an'l ta traafik reeel shite, issa thaa a beta whay upta tha mooterway?" I smile, sign and check the goods and aim to be helpful. "Worra ya wanna doo ista goo lift upta tha'end hear anna f'low t'rood round".

I always knew that my O level in gobbledygook and blarney would come in useful.

Just after lunch the first of many concrete lorries turns up. Like stampeding Bison you can hear these beasts from many miles away as they double declutch their way around all the local country bends. By the time the first one popped its head over the horizon we are all getting quite excited. Perhaps it's because pouring concrete into trenches symbolises a serious commitment to building that cannot be undone. This is it; the first part of the foundation and we are on our way.

Thanks to an overzealous soil engineer, the foundations soak up more Readymix and pound signs than expected. Talking to serial selfbuilders later confirms that the foundations up to dpc level is probably the hardest part of the cost equation since you cannot predict the required depth until you have cleared them pesky tree roots. At the time I remember being surprised that the remains of some footings found on an adjacent plot went down a mere two foot. The bungalow that stood there for about a hundred years survived two world wars and half a dozen thirsty willow trees. Still, we take comfort that our 1.8 metre trench foundation would probably halt the next glacier in its tracks if it so chooses!

The other thought which springs to mind is that I had originally planned to manage the filling of the foundations myself with the odd bit of shuttering. To their credit, Ron and Sandy eased the lava like flow around all sorts of nooks and crannies with no more than a shovel, a garden rake and a smallish piece of plywood.

The latter is especially important in order to keep the concrete lorries on what is called turnaround. This then takes advantage of any breaks in bad weather since rain and concrete do not make good bed fellows. Neither, it seems, do groundworkers and bricklayers, more of which later.

At the end of a hard day and even longer week I reflect on the lessons learned so far. Foremost is the crucial business of agreeing finished levels. As a layman, it's easy to get caught up in the egos of the tradesmen determined to have the last word.

My advice is to give responsibility to raising the foundations to dpc level to one contractor. If that involves him/her subbing out some of it, fine. The main point is one song sheet all agreed up front by all, none of the Chinese whispers that were still to come. The other gem of wisdom came from the groundies – forward planning with regard to access. I had delivered up front twenty tonnes of limestone when I only needed ten.

However, by buying more it costs less (per tonne) and more importantly the other half is used on the proto driveway to provide a firm access path from which to take delivery of goods, none more import than that initial Readymix concrete drop. With our mark very squarely made on this piece of sod we retire for the day and I scurry away to tell my mate (the biological one) all the news.

Monday 23rd March 1998

Major events planned for this week revolve around getting the blockwork sorted. And things haven't started well. Several hundred blocks (big bricks to you and me) were due first thing this morning. Apparently, this means different things to different people whereby eight prompt really means sometime after lunch. So I'm left with three hairy-arsed bricklayers sitting around burning my time and money cos there aint nothing to build with! Between them they've finished the crosswords in the Sun, the Mirror and now the Telegraph looks like going the same way. Then it dawns on me. Greenwich must have set up a new timezone and we're actually working on Buenos Aires local time. Time to hit the phone and express my disappointment in the language of the trade.

The builders merchants are sympathetic but the bottom line is that given a choice between a multi-million pound housing estate contract and a self builder we rate somewhere around rabbits in the scheme of things. Later on I seek and obtain compensation for me and my boys who are now shuffling around the oversite looking for mischief. Then one of those strange Karmic things happened which if you're a sad old hippie like me makes perfect sense. It goes like this. Head brickie is strolling around the oversite with a copy of the foundation design in his hands. He frowns and comes over. "Better check your drawings, boss," says he. "It don't match up". Alarm bells and a prolonged review of things show a blaring oversight on my part (boom boom). The suspended floor and the supporting blockwork don't and won't. Now you see the complete picture. Had the blocks arrived on time and work commenced we would have been seriously inconvenienced. Okay, cocked up.

I jump on my ageing motorcycle (the one that gets sold later to finance the kitchen) and head south passing the delivery lorry (avec blocks) en-route. Fortunately, Earthspan (as they were then) have their offices within 30 minutes drive. To their eternal professional credit and my gibbering relief the floor is redesigned and the production schedule amended at no additional cost either in money or time. Phew. Early afternoon and I'm back on site and the lads are hard at it. A quick conference with Barry (head brickie) and we're back on schedule. However, the smouldering mischief between groundworker and bricklayer is about to catch and I'm there to cop it. Barry is once again walking the grounds with a piece of timber and a tape measure in his hands. Words like "gauging" and "threshold" drift over and I am reminded not for the first time that when God created the world he probably employed a groundworker. Ever since they have the divine right to be right!

What is less well known is that God probably got a brickie in for a second opinion and to tender for the job. Groundworks are not only the single most important task in the whole build but the one job where the lines of responsibility get blurred. I'm a virgin builder and can only judge on what I'm told, backed up with reason, research and logic. He's angling for an extra course of bricks at cost (extras in other words). Naa, forget logic. Time to be as bullish as he's getting.

I explain what I'd understood from the ground worker about finished levels and even contemplate stamping my foot. Egos begin to get a tad chaffed and the letter of the law (i.e. our instructions to build) are brought out as Exhibit A. We agree a compromise. However, said ego is now bruised and I'm made to suffer. Every single course change I'm now summoned over to inspect and approve. Lessons learned? Same one as before about the responsibility for finished levels.

The other is, as project manager, one often has the dilemma of managing or getting bogged down in the detail of how things should be done. Ideally, we employ professional people whose advice we have to give at least the benefit of the doubt in the first instance. Trust is something you either feel after a period of time or you don't. The former has more risk and gets more rewards. The latter, everyone loses out.

Despite the bickering of two people who never met (Ron and Barry) I was fortunate to have well intentioned good advice throughout. But it wasn't easy. Anyway it's the end of the day; miraculously progress has been made in more ways than one!

Tuesday 24th March 1998

Good news, I've finished my homemade builder's box into which assorted cables and an electric meter will fit. With the promise of power I'm optimistically looking forward to Star Trek later that evening. Unfortunately, I've overrated the ability of the newly created, deregulated utility companies to talk to each other.

The farce that followed reads like something out of a Carry On movie. Four different teams turn up in no particular order. They all walk around purposefully, peer up at the pylon standing close by and ring HQ for instructions.

This keeps me and the Groundies (back on site with the JCB) amused for several hours. To a man they have Dayglow jackets and to Don's delight pristine Rigger boots. The best is left almost to last. Team A arrive in one of them lifting platform jobbies and fix a length of cable to what turns out to be the Live terminal.

Team B then dig a hole under the road and add a further length of cable (still Live as it turns out). Team C turn up look alarmingly up at the threatening sky (it's started to rain) and scamper up the pylon. So there's a live 440V three phase cable lying on a damp roadside verge. God knows how the postlady didn't get electrocuted. Eventually, sanity returns and a safe circuit is installed all the way to me box. Yippee hot meals, Star Trek and a supply of stunned wildlife.

BT's motto, on the other hand, must be that you cannot have too many surveys. To date we've had four. God knows where the actual line will end up and I'm beginning to look at last night's baked bean cans and a piece of string with renewed interest.

28

Breaking sod, or groundworks and services

Good news on the other front. Ron and Sandy have finished excavating the service trenches and a visit from Hot Lips, the building officer, is on the cards.

Monday 30th March 1998

Back after the weekend and a lot of persistent rain. I'm expecting the precast block and beam floor today and am thankful of taking Andy's advice about spreading four tonnes of aggregate around the site entrance. Lorries can get in (and more importantly out) and deliver the materials where you want them. Which, unfortunately, is where it went wrong. Barry is on site and pulls out the stops in getting one over on the groundie big time. Well that's how it seemed at the time. I'm advised to unload the blocks within the boundaries of the oversite.

The beams, on the other hand, are placed some distance away and stacked to about five feet high. In time I find out just how heavy they really are and the amount of extra effort this will entail. Here's the lesson. Always read and fully understand the setting out plans for the beams before the lorry arrives and try to locate the right sized spans as near to their final destination as possible. On reflection with all the rain we've had the marshland around the oversite would not have allowed things to be much better.

However, pre-planning with a knowledgeable helper is to be advised. I never really knew if the brickie had a motive or even if he thought he was helping. This comes back to the burning issue of delineating responsibility right from the start. Tomorrow beckons with a weights belt and hernia cream. Ask me tomorrow whether the few hundred quid saved by not engaging Earthspan to do it was worth the effort?

Tuesday 31st March 1998

I am awakened by the sound of early morning cursing outside the caravan and as I look through the caravan window I can see Ron peering up at a stack of beams taller than he can spit at.

It's a mess so the Hobnobs and tea are brought out. Some hard decisions need to be made. With one and half weeks grace less one bank holiday before the timber frame arrives the options are: wait till Sandy and his JCB get back from honeymoon (kinky or what?); delay the frame; or Ron gets out his encyclopaedic almanac of people with lifting gear. The latter wins the day and already it's costing me more than Earthspan would have charged.

By lunchtime the biggest crane I have ever seen on the back of a lorry turns up. Phew, this is the Conan the Barbarian of all lifters and the macho hormone rush I get goes somewhere to compensate those extra pennies spent (sad really). Joists are despatched some 20 metres hence and the roof tiles moved somewhere safer and away from the light-fingered Herberts known to frequent these parts. Marley tiles count as hard currency in these parts.

My purgatory is about to commence and no amount of Weetabix could prepare for what followed. Whilst the crane placed each beam within a metre of its final resting place they still needed to be edged across to allow the span of block work to be fitted. After three days of lugging blocks into the gaps my advice is don't. Pay someone, anyone, preferably someone built like an orang-utan with their own JCB.

On the positive side I know intimately how a B&B floor is constructed. I can certainly say I built or had a hand (or left a piece of mine) in almost everything, and my arms are bigger, longer and the squint I've developed doesn't bother me at all. Honest!

We now have a raised platform rising phoenix like out of the mud upon which a timber frame is destined to sit. Before the frame can be sited there's the little matter of placing scaffolding around the periphery to enable work to commence at an elevated level. What is known as the first lift is due first thing in the morning, about 24 hours before the frame is due. The other task is to fill any errant gaps in the floor structure with random offcuts and a dry screeding mix. This will give the whole structure a much more solid feel prior to the structural burden of the frame.

Lessons learned here include how having the right tool for the job makes all the difference. Angle grinder in one hand, caution in the other, I feel like Arnold Swarzenegger and set about the destruction of in-fill bricks like a boy with a new toy. I even get to wear toetectors! Unfortunately the glamour of the day only lasts till just after lunch when Grandpa Walton (father-in-law next door) turns up with his son-in-law in tow. I'm summoned over to inspect the communal foul drain we share. It seems that my groundworker in gaining access to the spoil heap has shunted soil sideways underground because of his JCB loaded weight. So the inspection chamber is now ovoid instead of round. It actually makes no difference to the functionality. But he's one of Yorkshire's spawn and clearly is angling for something. We agree to wait until a JCB can excavate a little before taking the matter to the United Nations!

On the main front things at this stage are tight but unavoidable since the next sequence of tasks are pretty interlinked and form what is known in management circles as a critical path. My past life in computing has taught me that success or failure often has a lot to do with identifying these tasks. My experience to date as a selfbuilder has taught me that grim determination and persistence in the face of apathy more often wins the day. Any delay in the scaffolding will directly hold up both the timber frame erectors and the roofing contractors.

Retiring for the evening we make our offerings to Murray, the patron saint of selfbuilders!

Good Friday 10th April 1998

Seven-thirty the next morning we are awakened to a sound that resembles a flock of crows outside the caravan. The scaffolders have arrived and before I've even blown the brickdust off the teapot a flatbed lorry and three of the happiest little soldiers I've seen on site so far have

31

already started to build what will be a familiar sight for the next few weeks. After the gaggle of miserable buggers we've had to date this is really refreshing. What's more is that they are self build friendly and positively encourage us in our efforts. But it gets better. Firstly, on discovering that our gas supply has run dry they effect a whip round from their own flasks so that office bound Mandy can have a cuppa. Then the head scaffolder spots the house bunny secreted away in the corner and we embark on a discussion about the merits of lop eared dwarves. This culminates in a barter of half a dozen scaffold planks (which turn out to be worth their weight in gold later on) for some nanky old timbers left over from the setting out.

By every turn this self build gets more surreal. Builders and the associated trades are supposed to be wind breaking ornery critters. Something weird has happened. Could it be new man meets builder's bum? Anyway, after an hour or so we have a stockade surrounding the oversite with the tiniest of gaps to allow the timberwork in and I begin appraise the playtime potential of all those ladders and planks.

Taking stock at this point I realise we are in reasonably good shape. We're about £1500 over budget but squarely on schedule. I wholly expected to lose some money here since the business of foundation work is so difficult to judge accurately so I plan to sleep well. More so since the missus is moving in at the weekend.

Chapter 5

Of chicken shacks, camels and new age travellers

Just before the more tangible parts of the build started to take shape (i.e. the frame and roof), Mandy put an end to my days of enforced bachelorhood by moving her warm and welcome body, plus modest home comforts into my distinctly sparse and decidedly male living space.

I remember having mixed emotions at the time. Having got used to my own company I had started to get odd little ways and, better still, an excuse not to shave.

The boys on site were in less doubt and noticed the changes out loud and in good humour from the first moment that air fresheners and toilet ducks appeared in the Portaloo. This then progressed to saucers with the morning cuppa and ended with a clean shaven gaffer happy that noggings were back on the menu!

With the anticipation of a particularly busy week ahead starting with the erection of the timber frame itself, I packed her off bright and early to earn the money which would put food on the table during the coming months. For my part the next few weeks saw my planning skills put to the test since at this point I had about four plates spinning, all of which were tottering precariously.

We had five days of frame erection, followed by chimney construction, squeezed in between roofing and a scaffolder intent on breeding rabbits. Enough said?

The framemen came from the west

At about eight o'clock in the morning the longest juggernaut ever to abuse a tranquil country road turned up. Looking like something out of a giant Meccano set it

33

had roof trusses and sundry timbers strapped all over the place. At the time I quietly wondered how it had negotiated the local hairpin bends around these parts without decapitating a member of the local pony club, or anything falling off. We had prior warning that the vehicle was on its way and that there had been some threat of a police escort being required. All of which added to the expectant drama. Somehow the trailer got reversed down the piece of sod we laughingly call our access point and a gaggle of men turned up in an odd collection of vehicles claiming to be carpenters of some sort. Most of them had come up from the bogs of Zomerset and spent a good proportion of their nomadic lives on the road, up ladders and chasing women. Well there was a goodly amount of mud around in those days, but I think probably the local gals were never really going to be on the menu. But they did know their job.

Have you ever watched ants? You know when one of them finds a crumb, gets his mates and before you know it there are lines of them working together co-ordinated without the slightest hint of any organisation. It gets done. Efficiently, like a well-oiled machine that has worked together on literally acres of wooden huts. It was these guys. The back of the trailer was stripped bare of anything light enough to be handled by lunch time and before long we had a small forest piled about seven feet high on the driveway. Just how the stack got to be that high still amazes me since not one of them stood a whisker over five and a half feet tall. Maybe they linked pinchers like the termites on TV.

Time to introduce the ants, sorry, cast. First there was Mark. Fresh from a messy divorce he'd thrown all his energy into being on the road, presumably to numb the pain. Unprompted, I was regaled with all the messy details within the first few hours of arriving. Next up Brian, master chippie with a gal in every port and the only man I've ever seen roll a woodbine with one hand! Then there was Sinbad, a 24 carat eco-warrior and veteran of countless road protests. With shaved head, tattoos and more piercing

34

to the inch than a Hell's Angel's belly button we fully expected the local community to give us very wide berth during the build. Which they did. Finally, there was the bloke what drove the lorry who didn't do much more than point out that it wasn't his job to help unload. I didn't get his name.

The main thrust of the day was to get the foundation timberwork in place on top of the suspended floor. This involved firstly checking the integrity of the oversite (foundation up to dpc) followed by the fixing of a wooden frame (known as a soleplate) onto the blockwork with special galvanised metal brackets and nails. Once this was all levelled off and square the remaining job was to lay and fix the individual frame components on top of the soleplate. Looking back it is hard to believe that the sheer weight of the eventual superstructure plus the appliance of a gas powered nail gun is all it takes to keep the frame in place but that really is the crux of it. Some of the panels are structural with many layers of timber glued together to form joists which I am told have the structural strength of steel. These are called glulam beams and are common to most timber frame constructions. But the engineering task it took to get them into place was nothing compared to the antics that followed.

Towards the end of day one Sinbad strolled over and enquired about any local barns he could crash out in for the night. Apparently the combination of saved cash from a bed and breakfast allowance not taken, plus months of living in trees had made sleeping al fresco a regular if not desirable state of affairs. The one thing I did know was that the local horse and hound brigade would probably call out the national guard and their muskets on sight of my eco friend. So as my site was bereft of anything suitable (on account of it being too comfortable) Sinbad went off exploring, via the local pub. A few hours later he was back, having met the enemy. Next he starts ferreting around in the hedgerow at the end of our plot. From our vantage point it was a bit like watching a wildlife program on TV without the sound effects. After a few minutes he discovers my nextdoor neighbour's defunct chicken shack, complete with feathers, chicken wire and some rusty corrugated iron. I soon understand why the boy builds timber frames since the resulting structure is a work of art. This was where he happily set up home for the next few days with Mandy leaving red cross parcels along our boundary each evening before retiring to the absolute comfort of our caravan which suddenly didn't seem so bad.

The next morning the team was on site bright and early and following a quick huddle over a cuppa a crane was ordered. At four metres plus, the main panels are far too heavy to lift safely into place by hand, so not for the first time in the build the village thoroughfare is under threat and I have to use all my years of management skills to stop the locals ringing the parish council to complain. Further, I have to find somewhere to hide a forty foot juggernaut without the use of mirrors. As it happened we need not have worried as painstakingly the frames were lifted into place and nailed to the sole plate. All this without a hint of a major traffic incident. Suddenly, all the angst of groundworker and brickie disputes were all worthwhile since the oversite was near perfect and with the exception of the odd gentle nudge with a sledge hammer it all seemed to fit together nicely.

By lunch time we had a giant garden shed where there used to be simply concrete blocks and by the end of the day the whole thing looked like the inside of an old church. Once again the enormity of the task ahead hit me. With a vaulted roof over the lounge and kitchen/diner some considerable effort would be needed to sort out the drylining and I made a mental note to ask the scaffolder's advice on the best options to deal with the height. Either that or I will have to put an advert in the paper for ex-trapeze artist who can wield a hammer.

Later that evening as Sinbad headed off to his poultry accommodation we skipped around the shell making plans like newly weds. At this point the structural components of the timber frame were visible. From the outside inwards the building would eventually have

36

several layers of materials starting with the exterior rendering (e.g. bricks, render or timber cladding) followed by a cavity gap, breathable membrane (in our case Tyvek), treated plywood, and the studwork itself. Between the studwork insulation material would be placed, with a vapour membrane and plasterboard completing the layering. The net results of such a design are superior thermal and sound insulation in addition to the construction benefits of speed and convenience i.e. no waiting while it drys or settles. At this point we could only see the promise, but it was still exciting, nonetheless.

The next morning the owner of nextdoor's plot turned up just as camp was being broke. To alarm calls from Mandy I was dispatched to distract his attention from the pierced and tattooed eco-warrior wandering nonchalantly across his garden. With rolls of polythene streaming out behind him this was kind of difficult. Fortunately, it was the son-in-law (the real owner) with whom I had had only about three words of dialogue to date. So I had to strike up a conversation out of thin air because if Grandpa Walton knew where the camp was he'd probably have a stroke, and that I didn't need. Life's rich tapestry rolled on.

Later that day fourteen pallets of facing bricks arrived at the same time as yet another of BT's hit squads. This could have been nasty. Quite by accident the bricks were about a metre from where they wanted to dig. I was reminded not for the first time that site management works best when you have all the information you need to plan ahead. I was amazed – it's all or nothing with these guys. Despite my insistence that a permanent phone line could wait until August, they still arrived to do the job. Best to smile sweetly and be grateful, it's one less thing to do later. As the week closed it was home to hot baths and colour television for the weekend, and catching up with friends and family all of whom thought that we had left the country.

We were on the final run of getting the frame finished the following week and, after a mighty refreshing weekend, we returned to what we Brits call inclement weather. It was threatening but not quite sure whether to rain or shine. So I decided to go for it anyway and take advantage of the fact that the scaffolding was still in place and set to with a paint brush on the fascia boards before the roofers covered it with felt.

About 4pm I had a call from a nice young lady from the BBC with whom I had previously spoken. Apparently a documentary was in the offing about selfbuilding in the UK and she'd like an in situ meeting to check us out. She eventually arrived about 5.30pm and at about 5.32pm so did Mandy who must have smelled the perfume of a single woman in the woods. This doesn't entirely surprise me since I was clearly a man of property, well, a caravan and a lot of timber. We chatted on and off camera (just a camcorder at this junction) and were put forward as prospects. Well that was it, now I was a luvvie and I proceeded to name drop the Beeb to all my friends. By the time the story got to the in-laws it was David Attenborough himself who had popped round and I could not wait to try out my thespian callings on Jewsons when I shouted up a bag of nails, darlings. Sadly nothing came of this impromptu audition due mostly to the advanced state of our build, we were told. Maybe it was the number of times I dropped "forsooth" and "upon my troth" into the conversation. Upon the close of the day I did take my good self to a place upon whence much slumber doth take place. Or to put it another way, we hit the sack, verily !

The next morning started briskly and before we knew it we had the bones of our new home laid out before us. Room dividers were now in place and we skipped from one to the next like kids. Co-ordination, or more accurately, juggling, now became the order of the day since the main structure of the chimney needed building up through the roof before the roofers arrive. We adopted a pragmatic approach to chimney design early on under the guidance of Barry by laying the bricks on the floor and imagining where the floor might finish. We then started sketching with chalk both on the floor and up against the emerging studwork. Based loosely around some features we'd seen elsewhere every completed level would eventually be viewed in situ, making decisions where any cut and tucks might look best as we worked our way upwards. I learned a couple of new bricklaying terms during this phase, fuelled in no small way by the competitive bickering between groundie and brickie. Ron was into the breech early on with a pre-emptive "okay, so ask 'im wot a King's Return is then", which then led to a counter bid of King to Pawn Four. I learned about corbelling whereby bricks are staggered across to reduce (or increase) the span of a row of bricks. This is especially useful when building in all those recessed nooks and crannies. I also learned how to break bricks lengthways and the shortest spans without resorting to the use of an angle grinder. Oh, they are called King and Queen's Returns respectively. This will be handy when next I have to split up something in the deep freezer. With a trowel no doubt!

To the sound of emptying gas canisters and rattling bricks in the mixer the day closed with three courses of bricks breaking through the ridge line. Technically at this point we had reached what is known as "Topping out". Sensing the euphoria and the beer in our coolbox Sinbad invited us over to his shack that evening for a return visit. Whilst I remember being uncomfortably aware that long dead chickens used to live here plus technically we were trespassing, the evening did prove to be a lively one. For a man a tad under thirty he had crammed in a lot of living. Somewhere amongst army life and destitution on the streets of Europe there was a pagan handfasting (marriage) in the Newbury Woods as the police started bringing in the dogs, before settling down in his current respectable vocation. Life in Middle England seemed kind of lacklustre after that lot. Not for the first time I reflected on how different people live their lives and pass through our own. Deep thoughts for the evening as we headed back to the utter luxury of our own shack.

Some good news greeted the morning. Firstly the late delivered blocks and subsequent rant by my good self yielded appropriate compensation. Barry was delighted and I wondered whether he really would have charged me for the delay. Still, he had vowed to make up the week's delay on doing the chimney, especially so since the roofers had now put on the felt and made it nice and snug. Funny thing, bricklayers like cats, don't like getting wet, poor loves. The other news was that the offending foul drain on Grandpa Walton's land now looked fine. We're now mates again until the next time I transgress which, giving my penchant for mischief, cannot be far away.

As we headed for the final lap on the frame erection I realised that a new record had been set with three teams of tradesmen simultaneously on site. I had also noticed that every trade seems to have its own timekeeping system and this reflects the stage of the build you are at. Earliest are always the ground workers who I expected anywhere between six and seven. Next brickies and scaffolders at quarter to eight, followed by roofers at any time after nine. Clearly the building clock starts from the bottom upwards.

That day we had brickies finishing the chimney, framemen tacking down the room dividers, and enter stage left the roofers. We'd kind of got used to the open roofed al fresco look so when the first rolls of felt started being unwound darkness descended. We had entered a new phase of the build. I was on double duty with regard to making tea today, especially so since the weather had at last changed for the better. The boys were down to their shorts and I began to notice that the village school run now seemed to include a slow meander past the site.

The weirdest thing, however, was the roofers. From the moment they hopped up onto the trusses neither man nor beast (nor maternal totty) it seemed would budge them until the day's toil was complete. Which was great for me but I did wonder how they made do for ablutions. Further, they barely drank any tea which is how the comparison to camels came about. Perhaps they slept up there too. After the chicken shack nothing would surprise me. Cloven hoofed or not, I was impressed with the rate that the tiles got laid. More impressive still was the rate at which the labouring half of the duo moved materials up there in the first instance.

By the time the lead flashing came into play I began to recognise a true technician on the ridge line. The boy was good, very good, and he knew his trade. Once again a trade recommendation, in this instance Barry had done us proud. Reflecting on their youthful cantering over the ridge line later that evening, I realised that this was one spouse assisted decision which made more sense in cold daylight.

To be honest I would have been up there roped up, beleighed and crampon assisted, with each row of tiles negotiated like the final assault on K2. Not only would it have taken forever but in light of the number of tiles that needed hoisting up there in the first place, several of my vertebra would have relocated sideways, halting the campaign in its tracks.

As I waved goodbye to the framemen I noticed the stack of useful off-cuts and literally sack loads of galvanised nails. All of which would get put to good use during the first fix. First, however, I needed to tidy up loose ends, not least the chimney breast detail, and a return visit from the good the bad and the surly.

Remembering how pernickety it all was with the foundation work last time, I had done my homework and sketched out exact instructions from the footprint on the virgin block and beam floor to each archway angle. Time well spent as it happened since they cracked on with little handholding and tangible sulking.

By the end of the day the chimney was looking good and the main arches and detail stacked up nicely. The real coup de grace came when the timber frame company got caught on the hop over the promised wood lintel to sit decoratively over my fireplace. Forewarned that the chimney was about to burst rudely into life they didn't have a piece of scaggy old sandblasted redwood to send me.

A few phone calls later, I had in my furtive little mitts the keys to the company credit card. Yes, they really gave me the number and the authority to spend up to £300 at the local reclamation yard. Before you could say the words 200-year-old kosher oak beam I was on my way to a well known yard in Cambridge.

I could have had it delivered but anxious that they didn't change their minds I prised it into the back of my trusty old Saab and headed back up the M11. Honesty and the threat of an abused suspension prevented me from throwing in a couple of neo Georgian marble urns. Which was strange in retrospect since the timber frame company went bust a month later. I wonder why?

Brickies are an interesting bunch and they have their own distinct pecking order. Barry (white no sugar) with whom I have the agreement is the boss so he has first dibs. Ray, late forty something, doesn't say much but drinks tea (black two sugars) for England and looks like little would surprise him after so many years of stacking bricks. Finally, there's Roy, the angry young man (white one sugar). Last one in, youngest and obviously still learning from the older brickies, Roy's burden in life is to do all the donkey work.

Occasionally, when one of the other two pauses to wipe a bead of sweat, Roy's in there with vigour, trowel swirling in the bonus break from the mundane before being beaten back to the wheelbarrow by the older boys. Football forms the main stay of the conversation punctuated by speculation about, yes, women. Since these are both subjects about which I know nothing (especially the later)

I resolved to do some research and quickly realised that footy is like anything else in life that requires a degree of bluff to get by. You only need to know a few words and a few key names.

"That Beckham'll do good," I venture. Disagreeing guffaws all round, it doesn't matter if they agree with you. I even ventured to suggest the boy might make captain. So much laughter. This is a true story and I'm still laughing.

The chimney was finally finished and I had the distinct feeling that there was as much pride in the boys as there was delight from us. The boys had done us proud and I took to showing everyone and anyone the new megalith in the lounge.

How many BT engineers does it take to change a light bulb? (answer – as many as you want!)

It was mid-May and another glorious day and what must have been the sixth or seventh BT surveyor loitering around the site. I had began to wonder at this point if they were bored, maybe they wanted to get involved? Who knows? I ended up telling him the same story I told all the others and he sloped away to await my later summons and I almost felt guilty doing so.

The brickies were frying up nicely in the hottest day so far and were amused by my attempts to slap sun cream on to my back unaided. I consolidated the joke by wearing a face mask whilst moving the cement about and learnt that all brickies are 'ard (with an A) and view skin cancer and lung rot as rites of initiation. I hope they're wrong. Still, we were cracking on and the garage wall was going up ahead of schedule due to another job in the offing next week. Most subbies spend their lives juggling two to three jobs at any one time depending on such variables as weather, delivery of materials and whether they like you or not. Mindful of this, I played dirty from the start and religiously plied them with regular tea breaks and best of all choccy bickies. They might be 'ard' but the sight of naked chocolate kept my boys loyal and, more importantly, on site. The bottom line here is as project manager it is your primary role to keep things moving forward. So unless your other plans are compromised by going with the flow, do just that and adapt the other tasks around their schedules.

The roofers were finishing off the lead flashing but due to a problem with the ridge vents we were being delayed. Looking back it is best to be philosophical under these conditions. Maybe its a Zen thing after all. Every time we got ahead or made the tiniest saving in the budget the cosmos decided to mess things up with supplier shenanigans and price hikes. At the end of the day I needed to cool down (in more ways than one) so I decided to scare my new neighbours by rigging up a makeshift cold shower out of sight underneath the scaffolding. Real luxury! Tomorrow evening we would be off to the local swimming baths who had yet to catch on to the fact that we spent two hours in the shallow end getting clean.

Every so often you have one of those days where everything tells you to stay in bed and let the day sneak by unnoticed. One particular day the portents started early on. I had good intentions to call off the cabling for my first fix. Things, however, went downhill rapidly as both the electric windows, air conditioning in the car and delivery date on the cabling gave up the ghost on the same day. What are the chances of that happening? So I took a detour to try and fix the car electric windows. I should have read the omens and remained stationary and out of harm's way as the gods were obviously trying to tell me something. First the car would cost lots to fix, the fridge in the caravan couldn't be cajoled into life and the brickie needed another five packs of bricks to finish the garage.

Oh, but it got worse. Part loads and a lead time of 14 weeks on the bricks made the durability of my stack of cement bags look decidedly iffy. I supposed we might turn it into a modern art feature just inside the driveway. Some good news before close of play, however, lifted my spirits. The roof vents which were mistakenly ordered above and beyond the needs of the build could go back at a cost of a 10% handling charge. The man at the local builders merchant has been a star throughout and has used his corporate clout to bend the rules in getting goods returned against the odds.

Whilst the rule "haggle till you're blue and trade the buggers off against one another" holds true, the relationship developed by using the same builders merchants for your business gives an intangible benefit only measurable as customer service. To cap off the day and quit while I was ahead I sprinted down the motorway to the suppliers before they change their minds.

Taking my lead from yesterday and mindful that no bricks means no brickies, I managed a whole thirty minutes lay-in the next morning. I then spent the later half of the morning ringing round for supplies of the now scarce brick since 14 weeks is unacceptable. The market forces kicked in on cue and I was offered them at £407 per thousand compared with the £267 I originally paid. I was polite and resisted the inclination to suggest where the bricks might be placed. The great thing about the build game, however, is that if, and only if, one guy doesn't have the product you need they will often suggest other suppliers. One such referral paid dividends and I was clear across the next county for five packs of facing bricks with a smile on my face. Better still, I managed to haggle a cheaper price than the original source. Small wonders at every turn. So I was on a run and after yesterday I figured the great builder in the sky owed me one. Next call was to the local electrical wholesaler who was out by £10 on the basic consumer unit. The interesting thing about haggling, talking percentage discounts never has quite the same affect as the genuine price you got from somewhere else. So I deducted a bit and cast back the lure. Most often the bite comes pretty close to the bid but not by much. So I recommend building in your own discount up front. As they say nothing ventured.

At the end of this phase we had the main structural components of the dwelling in place. The roof was on and the brickwork completed. I then had the task of completing the outside cladding (on the two shortest ends), plus all the fiddley bits involving mastic guns and lead flashing. So we come gasping to the lessons learned during this phase of the build.

Lessons learned

This is a particularly busy and critical time in the build program which will stretch both your planning and project management skills to the limit. More than ever it is important to identify the linked tasks and dependencies between the different trades on site. Communication skills come to the fore here with the need to pick brains for all the stuff you could not know at the beginning before making a coherent plan. Focusing on supplier lead times and ensuring that they know your plans and the importance of timely delivery is crucial. When suppliers let you down (and they will) be firm and professional in your handling of the situation. This is when using builders merchants as your principal source pays dividends since they have a good deal more clout in obtaining compensation than you.

Other specifics for this stage include :-

Co-ordinating the build of the chimney is important. Check the plans and needs of anyone who might be effected since no trade wants to hold fire and wait until another job is completed once they are on site.

Have a rough design idea of your chimney in mind before you start. In our case we knew the features we wanted to include and the sort of look of the breast. Most brickies come over all artistic when confronted with a chimney. Ask their opinion, remembering that in all probability they have seen a lot more examples of what works and more importantly what doesn't than you have. Picking their brains is not only flattering but probably the only chance most have to be creative!

We used the same facing bricks as the external wall with recessed jointing to create an aged rustic look. Another way of ageing the look of bricks is to let them tumble around in a (clean) cement mixer for a while. Cheaper than reclaimed bricks by far.

Double check with the roofers as to what you need to, and they are best to, supply. Some materials such as cement dyes they may have as spares from other jobs and you really won't need that much. Secondly, if the opportunity arises get them to measure up rather than relying on your own guestimate. Better still, do it together.

At the end of the timber frame construction there will be a lot of wood left over. Resist the urge to burn it (i) because it probably contains a nasty cocktail of copper, chromium and arsenic (hence CCA treated) and (ii) it will almost certainly disappear into the frame as noggings in the fullness of time. Mine was called CLS (Canadian Lumber Stock) and it is also very expensive. Likewise I had two large sacks of galvanised nails left behind which got used in all manner of external places.

And finally, remember to keep a sense of perspective. This is a particularly frantic time which will give you stress (if you let it). Whilst you are still only at the beginning of a long haul you have already achieved much through your efforts. Enjoy the euphoria of seeing it all take shape and delay chewing your nails down to the quick as a treat for later on. Oh, and smile occasionally!

Chapter 6

First fixing, now it's my turn

Summer was in full swing, it was June and there was an almost eerie silence about the place. Maybe it was because for the first time since we began I was on my own. More trades were due back later to do other things, not least to finish building the garage. However, since the build was being conducted on a "there's not a bucket load of spare cash basis", and the fact that we had pursued thrift with a religious zeal, things like the garage and any landscaping could wait until we knew better what was left in the pot.

Anyway, I'm a child of the seventies and my comfort blanket involved coffin sized speakers and giga watt amplifiers. This really was a lad in his own dream. I was in the middle of a plot and the only neighbours (and spouse) were at the office. Time for some sounds and all that stuff we blokes don't get to play loudly anymore. So I settled in for some Led Zepp and a lot of hard graft.

For the uninitiated first fixing is any activity that has to take place before the final finishes such as plasterboard (and by implication wall sockets), appliances, kitchen units etc can be fitted. I found it to be the longest and hardest phase of the build where everything seemed to take forever to complete. However, it is important to do the job properly since at this time the internal foundation for the more functional and cosmetic aspects of the build to come are set in stone. As a guide, first fixing is generally broken down into three main areas:

Carpentry - mostly involves fitting noggings and supporting woodwork. For me this also involved preparing two outside walls for cladding

Electrical - laying cables

Plumbing - pipework, electrical (earth bonding).

Carpentry and the noble art of nogging

I've always loved the sound of the word nogging'. It seems to conjure up images of something naughty in the construction game perhaps from the verb to nog. Well we have nogged (past perfect tense) and there is a lot more to it than first meets the eye. To put the thing in perspective this is the activity that focuses on getting the right supporting woodwork in place before a final surface or finish is applied. This can vary typically from drylining to external cladding, from mounting a smoke detector to hanging hi-fi speakers. A nogging (noun) is a piece of timber inserted between a supporting joist or framework with a specific function in mind. As a general rule this covers :-

– surface fixings
– services
– decorative support
– utility

The most labour intensive job was fixing additional support timbers in between the stud partition framework making up the internal walls of the bungalow, prior to the fixing of the gypsum plasterboard. This was a tiresome and long-winded exercise but one that could not be avoided if the dryliners were to be kept on schedule. Usually this means a lot of sawing up 38 x 89mm CLS timber into appropriate widths. These are then nailed at ninety degrees either through a convenient gap in the studwork, or using what is called skew nailing at whatever odd angle is possible. I picked up lessons on the best way to achieve this via tired arms, high quality cursing and bent nails. One suggestion is to pre-nail any noggings which require skew nailing before offering them up in situ. Another is to make sure you have the proper size and shape of nail (not as silly as it sounds), so you do not end up bludgeoning and splitting the wood into submission!

I also found having the right tools to hand helpful. Of these a crosscut saw, hammer, pencil and tape measure are essential. Two tips here. The first is to invest in an electric crosscut saw which will save you both time and aching arms. I invested in a Triton woodwork bench combination at about £300. The alternatives cost a little more but did not have the versatility of the Triton. This beast looks like something out of Thunderbirds or maybe Power Rangers (either way I'm showing my age). Its main feature is that it has the ability to turn into everything else. I don't think Virgil Tracy was ever intimidated by a spindle moulder though.

The second piece of advice is to use gauges. A gauge is any piece of material that represents a constant repeatable measurement. Get the picture? Cut the first length which should be a standard between centres measurement for the studwork (in my case 600mm) and use this to mark off subsequent lengths. The alternative involves a tape measure and a lot of wasted time.

It's obvious but vital at this early stage to make sure that the noggings do not protrude beyond the existing surface of the studwork, since this will incur the wrath of the dryliner when he has to plane or sand down the excess! Since we have a chimney breast to rival Stonehenge the areas where bricks met studwork needed special attention.

Bearing in mind that the standard size of a plasterboard sheet is generally 2.4m by 1.2m (roughly 8ft x 4ft in old money) and that studwork usually works out at 600mm between vertical centres, dryliners usually tack at 600mm and at the edges of the boards. With this in mind have a look at where additional support will be needed. If in doubt ask the dryliner at the time of obtaining quotes as to his or her needs.

Externally, I fitted feather-edged timbers to the two ends of my bungalow which we later painted black to affect a barn conversion look. This required careful thought about not only where to place the battens but also how to butt up against the brick pillars. Lead flashing work also needed careful thought since whenever timber meets brickwork either lead flashing or a dpc membrane needs fitting. All of which needed support timberwork in place. Again, check with the experts – the brickie in my case. Alternatively, check with your architect or building control officer if unsure. If you do plan to fit feather edged timbers make sure that you have decent ladders (two of them). Next, cut an "L" shaped piece of wood as a gauge for the distance between boards. Finally get hold of a friend who doesn't get vertigo when climbing up a ladder over six foot high. (Like my mate who didn't realise that the job involved climbing up a 5 metre ladder using one hand to hold the plank.) The alternative is to construct some form of scaffolding or sedate your helper (I jest).

Service noggings – There are two categories, electrical and plumbing and, as ever, planning is the name of the game, starting with a photocopy of the building regulation drawings. Next I marked out all the positions of proposed fixings required. This doesn't go into technical specifics at this stage but focuses on known positions of equipment that must have a supply (like the cooker, washing machine, refrigerator etc.) and the proposed position of all the desired outlets (that you know of). It's important to get the input of the other (voting) members of the household at this point since it's twice as difficult to change once the plaster work goes up. When we come to electrical installation this will get refined and revised further. Well, that was how it should have worked. What really happened was I declared UDI and ran amok with a bright red marker pen only to have my efforts critically reviewed by the finance director with the accompanying change request form. When you take into account the whacking great trade discount that is possible by negotiation, extra plugs and cable really don't add that much to the budget. So if you want triple socket outlets, why not? But do it now since extra connection points are much harder and expensive to add in later. Electrical noggings are needed in place for the eventual fixing of light switches, plug sockets, ceiling roses, smoke detectors, consumer and fuse box units, and transformer (possibly) if using low voltage lighting.

Light switches should be fixed at a convenient height. If in doubt have a look at someone else's house and have a measure up. I used the galvanised metal boxes (the technical term is pattress) throughout all my electrical fittings, though you can use the plastic push-through versions which negate the need for noggings. My thoughts up front concerned the stability of continuous pressure on the unsupported plasterboard. Make sure that you have to hand an example of the pattress in question and hold this up against the wall to check where the finished surface level will be. The alternative is gritted teeth if you find that the box protrudes beyond the plasterwork or that you need extra long bolts when you come to fix the switch plates to the pattress. Both lessons I learned the hard way. At this stage give some thought to how the supply cable will exit the pattress itself. Is it necessary to drill access holes for example out the back of the nogging? Without doubt plug sockets will receive the most wear and tear and I would counsel against the use of the plastic push-in pattresses in this instance. The use of a substantial timber nogging is more likely to protect against pulling plasterboard away from the fixings.

Ceiling roses require support by the fixing of a nogging between rafters. It is probably obvious afterwards but if you do intend to hang an all-in-one light and fan fixture, be especially aware of the weight and stresses involved and construct accordingly. Again think about drilling a central hole to pull through the cable work (which needs to be quite large for the three cables). Although smoke detectors (which are a building regulations compulsory fitting) will attach to plasterboard directly it is worth the extra work in putting something more substantial in place for all the times you have to press the test button and change batteries.

Early on in your planning it is a good idea to work out where the consumer unit will be and where the supply cables will enter and leave the unit. These are big cables and access will be difficult after the plaster board is in place. Consider the use of conduit (tubes etc.) to allow for last minute extras.

Low voltage lighting transformers need secure fitting. Often these can simply be the side of a rafter. I preferred to have my transformers raised away from the rafter to ease access and prevent possible overheating.

My plumbing system required surprisingly few support noggings, but principally around the boiler area and as utility supports (see later). Since pipework generally pushes through the studwork, the only real need therefore was the occasional pipe support. If, like us, you decide to fit underfloor heating make sure that you are aware of the placement of the manifolds (where the flow and return pipework meet) and any requirement to build boxes around it prior to screeding.

Once the plasterboard is in place it is too late to start thinking about shelves, picture rails, etc. Unfortunately that is when most of us realise our mistake. I've tried using a multitude of plasterboard Rawplugs to hang up shelving. Some of my walls look like someone has gone crazy with a rivet gun. The simple and wise answer is to overdo the fixing of extra noggings. Just as importantly is to make a note of where they are. If you have access to a video camera I suggest using it to make note of same. The use of bright coloured magic marker pens is especially helpful.

Start by making a note of the height and offset on the bare wood prior to insulation or plasterboard. Then record it. Here are some suggestions of where to place extra noggings for decorative fittings:

Picture rails – around the periphery of the room;
Bathroom accessories – loo roll holders, towel rails etc;
Hi-fi speaker brackets;
General shelving , bookshelves etc.

Long before the bathroom suite arrives it's vital that you work out the height of the screw holes on the w/c, bidet, bath etc. I had some very strange looks from the staff in B&Q whilst laying flat on the floor with a tape measure, the wife looking dubious noting down the measurements. But it did pay dividends when the loo slotted nicely (and very securely) into place. Additionally, think about the position of over sink accessories like plugged shaving box units. My personal favourite omission is extra support for the shower cubicle, be warned!

To save time I negotiated and bought pre-cut and sized door lining kits from my builders merchant. These come with two sizes of rebate already cut to allow fitting the header timber onto the sides. By simply reversing the header two widths of doorway can be catered for. The total length for the door lining is about five metres coming in three parts. These are cut to size and nailed within the door reveal (door opening to you and me) with the use of wedging to ensure 90 degree angles where it counts. I also cheated here and paid a man to do the job at the same time as hanging the doors (see chapter 7).

It is worth allowing support noggings around things like boxing in service pipes (soil, vents etc.). Kitchen units require special thought such as where the extractor hood hangs together with how the venting exits the building. If you plan to have the kitchen fitted by a professional check with them first as to the required position of supporting timbers. Likewise, check with plumbers and electricians for their specific needs.

Lessons learned

In all cases forward planning is the key to a good nogging session and the most obscure questioning of sales staff will save you a lot of hard work at a later stage. The type of material you use generally depends on what's available. My timber frame supplier left me a small forest of 89mm x 38mm CLS (Canadian Lumber Stock) timber after the frame was erected. This represents a large amount of money and it is certainly worth checking out when negotiating for your frame (if applicable). The final word is not to underestimate the amount of work involved. This task is labour intensive and takes a considerable amount of time (worthy of paying someone else to do maybe?).

Electrical

Electrical installation was actually something I looked forward to doing since I have been dabbling in a sort "I wonder how that all works" way with wires since I was a small child. Not much change there then. However, I was mindful that most people could not tell a RCD from JCB so I afforded the subject some healthy respect and did my homework. Here's what I learned:-

I suggest three must-do's before you decide how much if any to tackle. The first is to get hold of a copy of the truly excellent *The Which Book of Wiring and Lighting* by Mike Lawrence (Penguin - ISBN 0 85202 674 9). My first copy came from the local library and I quickly realised that the value of having a hands-on reference guide would outweigh the purchase cost. I suggest reading this little gem from start to finish skipping nothing since all of the major components and their appropriate applications are described in great detail. Just as important are the references to current IEE (Institute of Electrical Engineers) Regulations known universally in the trade as "the Regs". Although only as current as the most recent revision these relate the current recommended good practice and safety issues of which you must have due regard. The second must-do is to find a good local electrical wholesaler. Of course cost is an issue, but of greater value is the advice and help you can call upon when in doubt or just plain confused. I actually stumbled upon my local man through a trade recommendation. He's small enough to be helpful and hungry enough for my dosh to offer a healthy discount.

The third must-do is to retrieve the copies of the building regs plans made earlier and get hold of some coloured pens/crayons. These you will use to refine the initial wish list with regard to socket positions and cable runs. There is a fourth consideration you should make to get the whole picture. Ring up your local electric supply company which almost certainly through deregulation will involve about six different companies. If you can, find out their prerequisites for turning your builder's box (temporary supply) into a permanent connection. Hopefully, you will not get the inconclusive run about I encountered. The bottom line, assuming you can get hold of someone willing to commit to anything, is: installation and testing should (not must) be carried out by a card carrying member of the NICEIC. Tricky this one since most sparkies I talked to were members of the ECA (Electrical Contractor Association) who are in dispute with the NICEIC. Had enough yet ? I had. Here is what I did.

I kept on ringing electricians until I found one both qualified (either of the aforementioned bodies will suffice) and sympathetic to selfbuilders. The latter warrants further explanation. Throughout my build I have found two types of tradesman. Those who respect what you are trying to do and offer positive advice by the bucket load (after all they still get paid and who knows, selfbuilders talk to other selfbuilders). Then there are those who resent the intrusion into their world and lavish scorn and inertia on your efforts. Unfortunately, this is basic human nature. In my experience electricians and plumbers attract more of the latter type. Be vigilant and ask around. It's old advice but valid to ask the tradesmen you have used for references.

Having read the *Which* Guide mentioned earlier you will know the difference between a Protective Multiple

Earthing (aka TN-C-S) and a TN-S. Do they? Ask them which they think is appropriate then check with the local electricity board because they are specific to how the board connects you. My favourite white elephant concerns the use of multiple bonded earth requirements for plastic plumbing systems. One company wanted me to rip out half my studwork to add in extra wiring. Then I found my man who quoted me line and verse from the absolute up to the minute still wet from the press Regs. There weren't any requirements for plastic plumbing cross bonding (in my case). Whilst there are surprisingly few absolute rules (mostly they seem to be IEE best practices) I strongly suggest getting the whole thing checked before you do invite the board to connect you in the fullness of time. Once checked the sparkie will issue you with what is called a Partial Completion Certificate (they can only give full certification if they do all the work as well). This suffices for connection (although to this day no one has ever asked to see mine!!). So I had a couple of copies of the Regs drawings and a handful of coloured marker pens.

The installation starts with adding more detail to the initial schematic, starting with a simple key for all the components.

Symbol	Meaning	Identification	Comments
⊠	Plug socket	Single = Snn Double = DSnn	eg. S01, DS01
◯	Ceiling rose	L = ordinary LV = low voltage	eg. L01 LV01
◉	Light switch	SW = 1 way 1 gang DSW = 2 way etc.	
●	Smoke detector	SMnn	eg. SM01
▢	Fused connection unit	FCUnn	eg. FCU01
⊗	Shaver unit	SHnn	eg. SH01

I then labelled the first schematic "power circuits" and the second "lighting and other". I suggest one pair per floor. Next, I simply located the desired position of each socket outlet on the plan which, of course, tied up with the nogging' fitting described earlier (adding more noggings if required). This is the time to think about your needs rather than what a spec builder thinks is best for you.

For example, the disabled or infirm might consider locating plug points higher up the wall than is usual. By the same token there is little merit in using single sockets unless space is a factor. Utility areas such as the kitchen worktops merit some careful thought as to possible positions of kettles, toasters, microwave ovens etc.

If you plan to have under unit lighting or feature back-lighting in your fitted kitchen now is the time to think about the power sources. Particularly important at this stage is to make sure you are fully aware of the electrical needs for any heating systems you plan to have installed, if in doubt ask the supplier.

After being completely stonewalled by the heating and plumbing fraternity I pestered the suppliers of both my boiler (Firebird) and underfloor heating people (Nuheat) with technical queries on an almost daily basis. On both accounts they were helpful beyond the call of duty.

There are a multitude of power outlets the most common being the 13 amp plug socket. In some instances you will need to install a Fused Connection Unit (FCU) which as the name implies has a rated fuse located within the body itself, often this will be switchable with the ability to disconnect both the live and neutral terminals simultaneously (double pole). These are usually found as part of immersion heater or extractor fan circuits as a minimum but are often specified as additional protection on many circuits.

Again read the book and read it well. It is not my intention to list every combination of power outlet but merely to stress the importance of research and forward planning. Here is a checklist :-

1. Plug Sockets - Think about the possible position(s) of all your electrical appliances e.g. TVs will often migrate around a lounge over the course of time.
2. Check the power/safety requirements of all aspects of your heating systems.
3. Earthing - Check *and* double check the earth bonding needs of the plumbing circuitry. Plastic plumbing does not need earth bonding *but* gas and oil supply pipes do!
4. Cookers usually require between a 30amp and 45amp cooker switch. Installing the larger gives more options for the future even though the trend is for less current hungry beasts these days.
5. Specify external power supply needs up front since they require protection within the consumer unit and specific plug sockets and cabling.
6. TV/FM/BT sockets should also be drawn into the plan, again be generous.
7. Don't forget to add the doorbell or any security systems.
8. Get someone to look over the design. Women seem to have a particular talent for spotting our deliberate mistakes!! Nuff sed?

Lighting circuits were a tad easier to design and whilst there were a multitude of lamps coming on to the market at that time, the actual positioning remained fairly independent. Low voltage lighting, on the other hand, needed a hole in the plasterwork and somewhere for the transformer to sit. I used to find it irritating when builders would place ceiling roses next to the window.

So with the price of cable being measured in pennies (the only issue, really) place the lights/roses where it suits you. As with power outlets remember to specify outside lighting (patio/porch/security) at this point.

Now on to the exotic bits and pieces. Shaver units can be part of either a power or lighting circuit although the way the power is supplied will vary depending on which method you choose. My choice was to buy an integral shaver unit with a low voltage strip light, transformer (110/230V) and RCD (Residual Current Detector) protection. Smoke alarms are one of the few mandatory requirements. Miss these and both Building Control and probably your warranty supplier will close you down! I checked with the Building Control Officer about minimum distances from the different rooms in the house and planned accordingly. Extractor fans also attracted close scrutiny from Building Control. My blueprint specified an air extraction rate measured in cubic yards per minute, gulp! Well that had the electrical wholesaler scrambling for his slide ruler. If in doubt ask the Regs Office or fan manufacturer for a translation into English! While you're at it check the switching needs for the device. Mine have triple pole switches, impressed?

The final exotic is probably the room thermostats. My design came complete with recommended positions. Usually these line up with the light switches however there doesn't seem to be any standard convention about where to locate light switches so I suggest you visit someone and check out theirs. Alternatively, stand on one side of the door reveal (the opening) and close your eyes. Now where do you instinctively reach for a switch? Get the idea? Likewise, with cord pulls in the bathrooms etc.

Finally, at this planning stage you need to decide where to locate the actual consumer unit (or fusebox in old money) physically inside the dwelling. Also how will the supply tails (power cables) from the meter join up? Largely this will depend on where and how the temporary supply is in relation to the dwelling. I was advised in advance by the electricity company to have excess cable available (bundled up inside the box) to pull back later to the meter (which they supply). This saves about £150 in additional fees to reconnect cable ends (see how this book saves you money!). I decided to have the meter on the outside wall adjacent to the study. This meant hacking away at the brickwork to fit the big plastic box (you can only get from Jewsons, monopolies commission are you reading this?) and providing big bore conduit across the cavity wall. Since the actual cabling has the flexibility of a boa constrictor on Prozac I suggest you think this one through well in advance!

Now to pull the whole thing together. I was blessed with a computer and spreadsheet facilities. Otherwise some graph paper will suffice to compile a table which pulls together the information from the plans made earlier. Giving something like:

Device	ID	Rating	Comments	Tot.
DS	DS01	13A	Kitchen worktop	
DS	DS02	13A	Kitchen fridge	
etc.				
DS	DS32	13A	Bedroom 1	2
FCU	FCU01	5A	Control unit (Nuheat)	
FCU	FCU02	16A	Immersion heater	
FCU	FCU03	13A	Cooker hood extractor fan	3
Cooker unit	DK01	45A	Neon dual pole switch	1
CCOP	DK101	45A	Faceplate cooker con	1
Ceiling rose	L01	<150W	Main lounge	2
LVLF	LV01-LV04	20W	Ensuite master bedroom 1	4
LVLF	LV08-12	50W	Kitchen	4
CU	eg. Hager		2 way MCB/RCD split	1
CUCs	MCB	16A	Immersion	?
CUCs	MCB	32A	Socket circuits	?
CUCs	MCB	6A	Lights	3
CUCs	MCB	16A	etc.	
External	Porch	60W	Porch + 2 external	3
Other	Tape	Assorted	Insulation tape for labelling	6

Abbreviations: **DS**: Double Socket **FCU**: Fused Consumer Unit **CCOP**: Cooker Cable Outlet Plate **LVLF**: Low Voltage Light Fitting **CU**: Consumer Unit **CUCs**: Consumer Unit Components

It is worth considering adding a column for the power rating of the devices (as far as you can tell) and adding up the total theoretical power consumption for the dwelling.

It is unlikely that every device is likely to be in use at the same time and the electricity companies take an average which usually comes out at under 100A.

I raise this subject in case you have things like lathes or arc welding equipment in the shed which may trip out the protective devices in the consumer units. If in doubt check with your tame sparkie or electrical wholesaler.

At the end of the exercise you have a first cut shopping list for the wholesaler though it certainly will not be exhaustive. It's best to view the whole process as iterative with new components added as they occur to you.

To join the bits together, you can take two approaches – the cheeky one and the honest one. The first is to sidle up to the wholesaler or tame sparkie and ask them to join up the dots, this is the first test of your fledgling relationship.

The second is to research the rules (again read the book) and do it yourself. As ever, I pulled together the best of both worlds and amended a draft design to my needs. Two types of circuit design are generally used in modern installations, the ring and the radial circuit.

Sockets generally fall under the former with the supply cable running out from the consumer unit connecting up as many sockets allowed by the Regs within a specified floor area before returning to the originating spur on the consumer unit. Often these rings will pick up the fused connection units associated with cooker hood extractor fans and heating pumps.

Radial circuits, as the name suggests, go out from the consumer unit in one direction, picking up nodes en-route and terminating at the furthest point. Whilst lighting circuits are the most common example others such as immersion heaters and electric cooker spurs fall under this category.

Any outside power supplies such as to the garage or garden shed should also be radial circuits. The Which Guide suggests having separate circuits for the kitchen sockets and for each floor involved as a minimum.

Whatever you decide, join the dots with a different colour pen and keep accurate records. This not only makes trouble shooting easier but is of enormous help in testing and for any future amendments to the system.

I'll simply list my set up as a guideline. Please note that nodes are the total of all your sockets (double sockets count as one), FCUs and anything that allows an electrical appliance to be connected.

Circuit ID	Type	Nodes	CU Bits	Tape Colour	Other
			RCD Protected		
Kitchen sockets	Ring	10		Red	+Heating
Lounge sockets	Ring	6		Red	+Porch
Room sockets	Ring	12		Red	+Shaver
Garage spur	Radial	3		Blue	
Shed spur	Radial	4		Blue/White	
Spare					
			Non-RCD Protected		
Cooker	Radial	1		None	
Kitchen lights	Radial	6		White+Name	
Immersion	Radial	1		Blue/Yellow	
Lounge lights	Radial	6		White+Name	
Room lighting	Radial	12		White+Name	
Spare					

The above information should be lifted from the shopping list made earlier (e.g. DS01+DS02 etc) and you will notice the logical split between circuits labelled "RCD" (Residual Current Device) protection and non-RCD. This reflects the way my particular consumer unit was designed (called strangely enough a six by six split box). There are two types of protective devices in the modern consumer unit. The first which replaces the older traditional fuseboxes are known as Miniature Circuit Breakers (MCB). These are located at both the point of the external supply coming into the unit (the master) and at the starting terminal of each outgoing circuit cable. In addition a second protective device may be used which isolates the supply in milli seconds if you become part of the circuit or a fault occurs. These have varying degrees of sensitivity – mine is rated at 100mA and protects all the ring and external circuitry. It's a wise move to add extra capacity and simply use a blank insert where a MCB device would otherwise be located. I added one (i.e. two in total) on either side of the split for that attic conversion I might just start one day

Now onto cabling. Cable is usually flat and relatively inflexible. Often grey in colour it is different from flex, the white droopy stuff used to hang light bulbs from. Cable provides the connections behind the scenes (plasterwork etc.) and with the exception of two way switching is commonly referred to as twin and earth (TWE) with the live and neutral wires separately wrapped and insulated (i.e. red and black). The earth wire is left unsheathed within the cable. Economically, there is little point in buying cut metres since proportionally a reel of say 100m makes more sense to both the wholesaler and you! The sizes you will need are as follows (all TWE): Unless you plan to install stadium lighting ,1mm–1.5mm flex is fine for most lighting circuits; ring mains will use 2.5mm and cookers up to 10mm depending on power consumption. The other two types of cabling you might use are three core and earth, and steel wired armoured (SWA, aka Rambowire). The former is used (in this instance) in two way switching, the latter in protected external power supplies. That was the nuts and bolts of it all. Time to do the work.

Lessons with Obi Wan Kenobi, master sparkie

So there I am happily swinging Tarzan like from studwork to roof truss with lengths of cable slung casually over one shoulder when I noticed the delivery man from the local electrical warehouse at the window. Six boxes of assorted electrical widgets later and he's looking critically over my handiwork. He must be impressed, I figure, and engage in a conversation about folks who do it themselves. Strike one. Then the dreadful truth dawns; this man knows his circuit breakers. Strike two. What is more (or worse) he knows more than the bloke who sold me my raw materials on account of teaching him, his brother and the local head of Eastern Electric their trades as boy sparkies. Strike three and out. I am humbled and immediately beg forgiveness from he who shall be henceforth known as Obiwan Kenobi, master sparkie. Fate has dealt me a real ace here since a disgruntled ego is as nothing compared to 50 years of distilled wisdom sitting in your kitchen. The good coffee comes out and a casual yet purposeful interrogation begins. Here's the long and short circuit of it all with a few sparks of my own thrown in for good measure.

Lesson one
Establish a couple of what computer folk call buses, down the lengths of the house. Mine are called planks and they sit within arms reach behind my attic trusses.

Lesson two
Cut several six inch lengths of cable (using 2.5mm TWE) and fashion into loops held in place by a nail or two. Tack these along the planks (bigger ones here) and the trusses. Combining the two establishes a grid along which the majority of the circuitry can run. Inspection of your own circuit design will determine the optimum positions and obviously the more you have the easier it is when you start dragging through the cabling. Add to this any drill throughs required bearing in mind the structural considerations when drilling through rafters (always check with the supplier or Building Control if in any doubt). All of your desired connections will not lay exactly along the line but close enough to simply branch off nearby. All the above saves time, effort and money spent tacking individual cables in place. Obvious really (when someone points it out for you).

Lesson three
This concerns the location of cabling in relation to the final position of sockets. Try to keep spurs from ring main circuits to a minimum and always locate any vertical cable runs to within six inches to the left or right of the final socket position. That way you will always know where not to drill stud work. The same rule can be applied to switches etc. At the end of all this preparation your installation will not only be a dream to maintain and extend but will impress the pants of both the tester and building control officer. I suggest putting additional tags with text onto cables as they leave the consumer unit (where they are visible) and anywhere there may be confusion.

Lesson four
If you have studwork simply feed a thin batten through the middle of the cable roll and tack it across two studs near the consumer unit. This will allow cable to be drawn freely (like garden hose) when you are up in the attic. It also avoids cursing when cable snags and you have to keep on getting down the ladder. Now pick a circuit and start working away from the consumer unit. Remember that near the unit you will need extra clearance for both the incoming supply tails and the multitude of circuitry entering the box. TV and BT wiring follows the same logic with the exception that BT cable needs to be kept away from power cables because of electromagnetic pollution. TV/satellite cable generally comes with shielding built in. While you're at it consider installing a few hi-fi speaker wires behind the walls (mine even go into the bathroom, pure indulgence!)

Lesson five
As you begin to pull out cables to the final positions do two things: get a flipping great marker pen (mine's red) and write down the reference you gave it earlier, and most importantly give yourself a decent amount of pull through to play with (at least six inches). Also remember that ring mains simply go in and come out of the same terminals so

there is no real need to cut through but simply to trim back enough sheathing to make the connection. Lighting circuits daisy chain together so simply pull through about 6-8 inches of the three (supply in, supply out and switch) cables and do not forget to mark the switch cable differently to other two (I used red/white as opposed to simply white).

The one failing I did get a slapped wrist over was to ensure every earth wire had a green and yellow sleeving where exposed.

Lesson six
Adopt a colour scheme for each cable type. I used the following convention :-
* Ring main (2.5mm) - red tape
* Lighting (1.5mm) - white
* Cooker (up to 10mm) - yellow
* Immersion heater (2.5mm or more) - blue

Lesson seven
Invest in the right tools for the job. As a minimum this should be :-
* Wire strippers - The 'automatic' strippers sold by Screwfix are excellent but really aren't man enough for the job! I wore out and returned two pairs. However the concept and time saving is still worth thinking about. Alternatively, ask your wholesaler for something a bit more industrial.
* Neon screwdriver – These work by making you part of the circuit with a whacking great resistor inline to prevent getting a shock. This sounds more alarming than factual but unless you are adept with a multimeter that little neon light tells you what you need to know when you need to know it!
* Pliers with insulated handles - used to cut cable and twist the ends.
* Claw hammer for banging in retaining clips and for wrapping around the end of runs when some extra leverage is needed!

* Mains powered (or seriously chunky cordless) two speed chuckless drill for drilling through studwork etc.

* Decent 22mm or more drill bit. I used an American spade bit which was easy to resharpen but sometimes bludgeoned more than cut! Ideally, get a good quality coredrill bit since the amount of work it will do (even in the plumbing) will justify the expense. Think about TCT to save constant resharpening.

* Coloured insulation tape - As detailed in the table used to tag the visible cable runs (and yes it is worth the effort). I checked with a couple of sparkies for some sort of industry standard, what you see is what they said, and what I did.

* Stanley knife - No self respecting selfbuilder should be without one.

* Tool/utility belt - You know the sort of thing dad gets for Xmas. Made of suede get one with a cordless drill holder if possible. I had to surgically remove mine from my neighbour so impressed was he!

First fix plumbing
(or the secret brotherhood of plumbers)

By the time I'd got around to plumbing I had one of those moments best described as a "blinding flash of the obvious". We've all heard of trade unions, we've all probably heard of the Freemasons. All noble organisations in their way, I dare say. You might even rejoice at the thought that the days of closed shops were dead and gone. But I tell you what it's nothing compared with the "secret brotherhood of plumbers". Not so much a closed shop as a conspiracy to keep the noses of uninvited members of the self building public away from their holy books. Throughout this build my approach has been to read and research whatever is involved in the next phase of the build. With all the tasks I conducted an overview (for budgetary and planning purposes) about a year before, and followed up in detail a month or so before we started. However I took the view that anything concerning utilities should be looked at in detail up front as I knew that it

68

would have implications and knock-on effects later. A good example of this is where many disciplines meet such as heating. Heating takes in electrical work, some carpentry, fuel supply, many building regulations and, of course, plumbing. So my brief in the first instance was to find out what was involved in specifying a heating system followed up by what trade needed to be involved i.e. how does it all fit together? My aim (as the rule I repeatedly state throughout this book) was to determine how much I could and should do myself. A simple premise you would have thought. Think again. I started with a trade reference in the yellow pages and spoke to someone claiming to be the helpdesk. (Like yeah!). I've managed to work out that the core question concerns what type of fuel you plan to use which implies a particular type of boiler and so on. It goes something like this. "Hello I'm building my own home (big mistake saying that) and need to plan the design and installation of my heating system, can I ask you for some advice, a couple of questions maybe ?" Pause. "Are you a plumber?" "Er no, I'm building the house myself and just need to get a basic understanding of what's involved so I can decide how best to proceed". "Sighs, tuts, so you're not a professional plumber then ?" Sighs again. "You know people go to college for five years to learn how to do this properly, there's all sorts of technical stuff you need to know, special tools and techniques and it can be quite dangerous for the amateur". "Yes I realise that, which is why I need to make sure I understand the basics, you know, the main components, statutory stuff, safety etc, and where a specialist needs to be employed".

Shuffling papers at this point. "You need to get one of our members come around and assess your needs, then they'll design and install the whole thing for you". "Okay, so that will cost me money before I've even decided what system I want installed". Maybe I'm not explaining things properly so I persist. "I have some specific requirements in mind for example will they have knowledge of how solar panels can be incorporated or whether condensing boilers are appropriate for a small family which uses a lot of water". We've reached the end of the road now so. "I'll send you a copy of the members in your area, we don't just give information out willy nilly you know". There it is the real crux of the matter. "Thanks for your help, click".

This was a pattern that repeated itself with every variant on the theme of heating engineers no matter what I tried the door to the inner sanctum was slammed in my face time and time again. Maybe I need to learn the secret way of holding a stilson to be recognised by the brethren. Was it personal I wondered ? No, I realised coming full circle to a blinding flash of the obvious, it's good old fashioned human nature protecting their own interest. The really sad thing was that on the rare occasions I found a professional willing to help without any promise of financial reward, I inevitably ending up doing business with them. After all if they are self assured enough not to be threatened by the persistent questioning of a boy builder then a) they probably know what they're talking about (and I always double check information gleaned in this way), and b) experience has taught me that business relationships built on a degree of mutual openness (and in time trust) have the best chance of being successful. Bottom line, I like to know what I am getting for my money and the man that is comfortable telling me just that, has my vote. Which was how we broke the loop of what boiler, what system, what design and who does what.

One of the better decisions we made was to install underfloor heating and by chance hot on the heels of the above conversation we met the marketing director of NuHeat at the Self Build show at Alexandra Palace. I have shamelessly plugged NuHeat throughout my writings and with good reason since their help desk in Devon really was just that. By the end of our installation I was on first name terms with most of the staff down there. NuHeat conducted a capacity plan for the size of boiler and the energy storage device we would need. They also recommended a couple of boiler manufacturers and designed every last inch of the underfloor pipework. Bless them one and all. Working out where the above floor pipework went, however, was a little more erratic and down to yours truly.

Before I started this lark I naively assumed that everything would have a specific design brief with well laid out guidelines on how to do things. This naiveté is compounded by the fact that I come from an industry (i.e. computing) where the problem is not so much that there are no prescribed methods of doing things but that there are too many ways of doing the same thing. Further, like the electrical trade described in the next chapter, nobody can agree a way to standardise the approach. Anyway back to the problem in hand and how to design where the pipework will all fit.

Before launching into what I actually did perhaps some plumbing fundamentals might help:–

* The common size (diameter) of pipework employed in domestic installations are 10mm used mainly in fuel oil supply and small bore heating systems, 15mm, principally used to connect the actual appliances (sink taps etc.) to the main supply, and 22mm which usually carries that supply and acts as the backbone of the system. The larger bore 28mm tends to be used around the boiler itself, mainly around the flow and return manifolds.

* Nowadays there are more options for the material used in pipework than in the past. Essentially it comes down to copper and what is generically called plastic piping. The former has the advantage that it is relatively cheap, widely available and the traditional plumber's first choice. The downside is that it is inflexible and so runs in straight lines into angled connectors and usually involves soldering work to connect together. It is possible to use what are known as compression joints which simply require common sense and dexterity with a monkey wrench but at a relatively higher price than soldered joints. The great advantage of plastic plumbing is its ease of use involving no more than a snip with specialist cutters, a reinforcing pipe insert and firm push into the special (push fit) connectors. The only downside I can see is the expensive nature of the material and the reluctance of traditional

plumbers to use it. This seems to add something to the taking the horse to the water syndrome. Despite my reservations about the plumbing trade as a whole, they do write a good safety specification and in all the cases applicable to domestic plumbing the product passes with flying colours – with two exceptions. The first is around the flow and return manifold of the boiler itself and the second in the supply of non-hydrous material, e.g. heating oil, for which it is unsuitable. The clever builder quickly recognises that cheap copper pipe can and will (legitimately) connect with push fit plastic connectors which in turn are cheaper than compression joints. You decide for yourself.

* All plumbing systems start with water entering the dwelling through the rising main (usually located under or near the kitchen sink). The route the water now takes depends on whether you opt for a direct or indirect system. A direct system feeds all of the cold water outlets (e.g. taps) directly from the rising main. In our case it also powers the hot water system (heating and domestic supply) at the same (ish) pressure that it flows through the rising main. This approach is more common and favoured in Europe, whereas it is viewed as heresy in this country. The advantage is that it requires no coffin sized storage tanks in the attic and no additional pumps for showers etc. It does, however, rely on there being a minimum head of pressure maintained by the water authorities. At the time of going to press they would give no commitment to pressures. The downside of this system is that lack of guaranteed pressure. Since my underfloor heating system only requires one bar I've not lost any sleep.

The other thing to consider is the availability of supply – if the water is turned off you have no storage. Indirect should be obvious now. This is where water is supplied to one or more storage tanks high up (to maintain pressure) in the attic which in turn supplies both the cold taps and heating systems.

In design terms a cold supply can simply fork out tree-like from one tap to the next. Bearing in mind that each drain on the source will reduce the pressure, it is worth thinking about where the supply is most crucial. For us this was to supply the boiler and shower. Our hot water system runs from the flow manifold on my energy store and describes a loop which is pumped as part of the circuit to ensure hot water is always available. In fact, the great advantage of our system is that it is almost (we've never done it yet) impossible to run out of hot water. As a young family a seemingly endless supply of hot water is important. I believe that this can be a problem with some designs of condensing boilers. This last observation highlights the whole problem with the heating/plumbing industry and it is my belief that the brotherhood are in for a nasty shock with the advent of more and more people like us asking questions and having a go. For instance, the two most fundamental decisions you make about the heating system are: what fuel and by implication what type of boiler? Technology has moved on quite a bit over the last few years with great leaps in both efficiency and the choice available to the buyer. If we bought cars with the same blind faith that the plumbing/heating trade seems (from my experience) to expect then we deserve what we get. However the 21st century consumers quite rightly want to know what they are getting for their money, none more so than selfbuilders. Well that's my view and my soap box anyway. To bring this rambling to the point, boilers and the design of system they imply must be chosen by looking at the user's requirements. Some, for example, are very efficient but have a smaller storage capacity. In a high and frequent demand for hot water scenario (i.e. grubby kids at bath time) we need to know this. Likewise, how long will it take to recharge the supply once the kids are scrubbed? So our requirements were for efficiency, volume, fuel type and ease of installation in that order. All this added up to an oil fired boiler (with an efficiency of 80% plus) linked to NuHeat's proprietary energy storage cylinder which in turn acts as a reservoir of hot water for both the underfloor heating and domestic supply (more of which in the next chapter). Longer term, when we have enough money and

73

energy to take on the planners when we plan to add solar panels to the equation. As you might have guessed, for materials I employed mostly Speedfit plastic plumbing by John Guest whom I often describe as a god for making basic plumbing accessible to the public. I first thought seriously about using plastic plumbing after visiting a fellow selfbuilder who at the time was building one of those Beco (foam and concrete) dwellings and had used the product extensively. They had even managed (as luminaries of the Association of Self Builders) to talk someone from the company to come down and give the local group a seminar on the product. Talking to other sufferers (self build co-dependents if you like) is just as good an idea and one that I heartily recommend. If nothing else, it makes you realise that you're not alone and it gives you access to a lot of wisdom out there, things people learned the hard way so maybe you don't have to! Getting onto John Guest was one of those moments where a problem I'd been grappling with became very clear and I owe Graham a debt of thanks. The trade, of course, thought otherwise with comments like "Oh it's untried technology, surely it will melt, best stick with what works in the field etc". The irony was that the major utility companies (both water and gas companies would you believe, though not for gas) had already endorsed its use and had stress tested it up to some ridiculous extremes.

Of goats and stopcocks

I mentioned earlier on in this chapter the need to be aware of the utilities requirements. I nearly dropped a right royal brick over this one, so pay attention. Water, I supposed, got laid to a tap (called the site supply) which then got connected to the incoming pipe which the groundworkers put in place through and under the foundations to the rising main. Sounds a straightforward assumption doesn't it ? Well, of course, it wasn't. Getting the supply is fine but there are two areas where the local water authority inspector needs to give the nod.

The first is the way that the supply passes through the foundation (it has to be insulated and rat proofed); the second, however, concerns a whole gaggle of regulations. Which is how I first met Mr McGinty. Maybe it's because I'm a writer but words amuse me and the images they convey even more so. By the time he arrived I had a mental picture of an Irish goat from a well known Val Doonican song very squarely in my mind's eye. As it happened, Frank was nice bloke in an officious, puffy sort of way. But once I had acknowledged (and bowed) to his encyclopaedic knowledge of regulatory widgets we were on first name terms and the best china. There are many things you need to know about the way the pipework is put together. Whilst these are beyond the scope of this book they should not be viewed as intimidating nor beyond the wit of selfbuild man (or woman).

Mostly this concerns the placement of stopcocks, non-return valves and the threat of what is called back-siphoning. This is where used (or contaminated) water can enter the water supply by a reverse pressure drop, best exemplified by thinking about a hand-held shower attachment on the bath taps left under the water.

The wise self builder asks for a contact number of the area inspector at about the same time that the initial site supply is laid on to avoid any nasty surprises later on.

Looking back, I was very fortunate to have a visit when I did, since I had already installed (incorrectly) the rising main supply behind plasterboard and would never have been connected without the man (or his goat's) approval.

Be warned: be nice to inspectors and be persistent in finding out when their services (i.e. inspections) are required since this is often information that is not freely offered when first you make contact with a utility company. Here endeth the lesson with a summary :
* Know what is needed from a statutory point of view asap.
* Compare the prices of plumbing materials and make sure your builders merchant can supply them.

* Use the building regulations drawings as the plan for where you lay the pipework.
* Buy the correct tools for the job up front.
* When approaching any potential supplier of a system have a list of your requirements prepared up front. Ask questions if you're not sure; after all it's your money and you only install a plumbing/heating system once so get it right and get it right for you not what the tradesman wants.
* Consider breaking the job down into work that maybe you could do comfortably into the more specialist stuff that needs a professional's touch. For example, drilling holes (once you've checked the specification) in your rafters and even pulling through pipework is not beyond the wit of most people, but it is labour intensive (so it costs you money). Obviously, you would need to agree with the tradesman as to the how and where and the division of labour.
* If the whole process scares you or maybe getting up ladders isn't an option leave well alone and pay someone. Likewise, do not take any risks you are not happy with.

Epilogue!

The footnote to this particular phase of the build is to think back to the Glastonbury festival of 1998. The weather ? The mud ? Yes, we were there. Not content with living on a building site we decided to go and roll around in the mud in Somerset. Which was a bit like coals to Newcastle except we brought back more mud than we took! We also opened up our home to the curious folk (as in interested people) of the Association of Self Builders one warm Saturday afternoon. Maybe we hoped to catch a few of them before it was too late (only joking ?). Either way we were ready for second fixing. And so we arrive panting and gasping at the end of the second fix with cables, pipes and studwork glaring at us to finish the job. Second fixing beckons and with it the anticipation of some very pleasing feelings of moving on to the next phase.

Chapter 7

Second fixing – down to brass taps

There's something quite exciting about recognising that the second fix is under way. I don't think that it's anything to do with an imagined glimpse of the finishing line although at the time it might seem that way. No, I think it's more to do with a feeling that when we start screwing a light fitting onto the wall or start to line up the actual place that the loo will finally sit, we have a sense that this is it, no more faffing around with bits of timber or cement that nobody will ever see, this is the final resting place. Hopefully, whilst the finishing line is still some miles off (with more than a few hills along the way) we have turned the corner so maybe it's okay to tighten up that multipurpose suede tool belt from Xmas and set the your chin in a meaningful and determined grimace before stepping up to the crease. Next turn to the nearest nogging and mutter: "So ask yourself, do you feel lucky?". Too many late night films, obviously.

As with all the build to date there is an actual batting order (critical path) to the forthcoming weeks sport and it goes something like :
* drylining
* electrics
* plumbing
* carpentry

The logic of the above should be obvious. Initially, we need plaster(board) on the wall to fix things on top of before attaching plug sockets into which plumbing/heating components can be connected. In truth, the plumbing and electrical work can occur in parallel since they are often interdependent on one other. Finally, the cosmetic (e.g. architraves) and functional (kitchen) aspects of the woodwork can be tackled.

Drylining – A couple of good old boys from the fens

I choked on my muesli the day drylining started since Grandpa Walton next door had done me a good turn and recommended a man from deep in the wetlands of Norfolk as a potential dryliner (which is kind of ironic). Now that really had aroused my curiosity since the one thing you could say is that either by uncommonly good luck or some latent ability he did seem to get hold of some decent tradesmen. What I really wondered was what sort of divine creature could ever live up to mark and get employ with the man himself. Grandpa Walton is a devout church goer and I wondered whether the local vicar had a little side line to raise funds for the church roof (it's always a roof isn't it?).

To put things in perspective, I'm reminded that the official family chippie (or Tom the Baptist as he's known in these parts) walked on water before coming here. But then he lives the other side of Ely where it is all below sea level! Also Tom turned out to be a likeable normal bloke. Perhaps paranoia has come to live with us along with the rats.

So I met John and his mate, also called John. Since neither stand a whisker over five foot three I quietly wondered how plaster boarding measuring eight by four would ever feel the warm embrace of my studwork. Just to confuse things not only were they both called John but one had a dog in tow with eyes the same colour as David Bowie's. You know, one blue one brown? What is his name I wonder? Ziggy ? So we have John the boss, John the mate and Ziggy. Then it dawns on me the dog is part of the team. Perhaps he holds the boards in place whilst John and John leap up and whack nails into place. I need not have worried since somehow what they lacked in height they make up in upper body strength and dexterity. Better still the boys drank tea like it' was going out of fashion. A level playing field at last. In no time at all sheets of plasterboard were being manhandled into the house and a patchwork of inner cladding began to take shape. This was one of those tasks that I had always kept on the reserve list as jobs that I might pick up if things got tight financially. Watching the two Johns in action I reckon I could have done the job but, and it is a big but, it would have taken me three times as long. Furthermore, there was no way that I could have manhandled the boards for the ceilings into place on my own. I did research this particular task in quite a lot of detail. I even spoke to some nice people at British Gypsum regarding the appropriate tools and techniques for the job. Just for starters there are board lifters for the ceiling and the walls. There are even specialised tacking devices, plus copious notes and widgets on how to achieve the perfect finish (i.e. taping and filling). When you add it all up the sum total of tool hire and cock-ups you (well I) could make on something that is visually in your face, is it worth it? I thought not. Many sins can be hidden behind panels and the structure of the house. Something as obvious as the inner walls simply aren't worth the risk. That was my view and one that got reinforced at every turn as J&J&Z strutted their stuff (all eight legs of them).

Lunch time arrives and the boys settle into their packed lunches. It is always difficult to know whether your company is an intrusion on site during a break in works. My brickies left me in no doubt about things from the start and it's a wise site manager who honours the odd moments they need to have a break from things. Usually that includes the scrutiny of the boss. Being the perceptive sensitive type, Grandpa Walton next door never really cottoned on to this basic premise and I often heard his subbies complaining about being pulled around site during lunch time to inspect something that wasn't up to spec. John, John and the dog tolerated and encouraged my company from the start and after many weeks of working on my own I was glad of their company. It is a wise man, I believe, who listens to another man's story and I remembered hearing of how Winston Churchill used to do the same. One story goes about concerning a man who used to make glass eyes sitting next to the esteemed statesman. After all the pomp of state banquets I can only imagine what a refreshing change that must have been. It's also a wise man who doesn't prejudge another man's wit on the basis of the job he does. Not for the first time I am intrigued and thoroughly enjoy the cut and thrust of a sharp intellect or two. Today, quite unprompted, we are discussing Europe and the pro's and cons of entering into the single currency followed by the value or otherwise of having a commonwealth. Over the hour's break we culminate by simply talking about the local wildlife. John the dog is something of a wildlife nut and reels off the names of the local bird population without taking a breath. True to tradition I also get to know all about their domestic woes and wives. Great stuff.

Three days on and all the boards are up, tacked and seamed. Suddenly, the open plan vista has gone and we now have rooms where previously there was studwork and gaping holes. Cablework now hangs out and demands sockets be attached and fixed in place. Likewise, assorted pipework. Even better the acoustics in the lounge just got better. So in anticipation of another period of solitude I scuttle off in search of loud vinyl to ease the coming weeks.

First fix childbirth

News of an even bigger change to the project arrived about teatime along with a bottle of wine. It was October the 8th 1998, our wedding anniversary in fact, and instead of something straightforward like a pair of socks Mandy presented me with a lolly stick with two thin blue lines across the bottom. No it wasn't an ice cream. This brand was called "Predictor" and suddenly we have nine months to deliver the project!

The house build took on a new direction at this point not least of which was the business of getting out of the caravan and into the half finished bungalow before we needed hot water and cotton sheets. The bungalow at this point was weatherproof but spartan. Over the next few days I came up with all manner of compromises in getting the home reasonably comfortable. Suddenly, bits of plywood were doubling as bedroom doors. An electric supply cable now dangled across attic trusses and the en-suite was connected with a garden hose to give us a flushing toilet. The lessons learned on drylining pale by comparison. But here they are anyway. (Where's that book on DIY midwifery?)

1. As ever, get the contractor to estimate the amount of plasterboard required. This will include an amount for wastage. Be aware that there are two types of board depending on the type of jointing you will use. These are feather edged and square edged. The former is used when tape and filler is used and has a rebate at the edges to take the filler. Also be aware that the type of finish you plan determines which way around the boards are tacked in place. One side is called grey the other white.

2. Make it clear to the builders merchant that excess boards (subject to condition) will be returned.

3. Places like recessed windows will require Artex cement so have a couple of bags included in the order.

4. Ensure that all the delivered boards leave the depot and arrive on site thoroughly wrapped up against the elements. Inspect these on delivery and have any variances noted on the delivery note. This is especially important if you have to return any boards.

5. Make sure that access to difficult areas can be achieved safely and that your contractor is aware of this from the start. We have four metre high ceilings in two of our rooms and the trestles plus scaffolding planks bought earlier were used to reach the giddy heights.

6. Bag up all the waste materials immediately. Plasterboard is one of those materials that is a nightmare to get rid of once it gets wet so leaving it around the site for later disposal is not an option. Bribe the dustmen or visit the local tip but get it off site.

Second fix electrics - Return of the Jedi
(or board wars maybe?)

We have to fast forward at this point in the story since it is now January 1999 and Mandy has started bubble netting in the local swimming pool. You know whales and all that jazz. Greenpeace is on hold until May and whilst she can still walk I'm still putting her to work in the bathroom painting the bare plasterboard. Christmas came and went with an off-site over wintering at my mother's house. There we indulged our new found passion for hot baths to the max. So we were clean and mean and ready for more. My penance was now the beckoning second fix electrical work.

In total there must have been three miles of cabling in and around the loft and wall cavities plus about a hundred assorted plugs, sockets and ceiling roses sitting in boxes glaring up at me. But I was prepared to fight dirty.

In my left hand, the plan of where everything went together with its own special name tag. In my right, the big six shooter that has built the very fabric of this house – the cordless drill-driver; it was time to get busy. The little scraps of paper detailing how things fitted together had become an integral part of my life by now and they are still kept together in the big blue book where everything that is important about this build is kept. Although threadbare, I could still make out the early musings on how to break down the home into circuits.

I decided to tackle the kitchen first where the largest collection of plug sockets was found. If I've done my job correctly then between the autostrippers and electric screwdriver things should go smoothly. Which they did up to a point.

The point was that I tried to make sense of what the electricity board actually wanted from me before they would make us live. More of which later.

I believe I am pretty thorough when it comes to anything involving risk. None more so than with electrical work. So I had worked out a natty little way of testing before inviting anyone more formal on board. Initially I used a number of smallish batteries and a torch bulb to check continuity (i.e. no breaks or shorts in the circuit). However, the resistance of 1mm to 10mm cabling is well beyond the ability of the average Duracell bunny. So we focus on the pragmatic. First off I bought one of those plugs that you simply put into the socket which indicates whether there is a problem or not.

Next, aware that I have a builder's box with a flipping great earth rod sunk into the ground, I started to think about how I could use the built-in safety devices to conduct my own fail safe testing. I also have miniature circuit breakers (MCBs) which are the modern day equivalent of fuses with the advantage that they don't blow (or burn out) but simply switch off. The best bit of all is that I have Residual Current Detectors (RCDs) in both the builder's box and in my newly installed consumer box. So in total I have a system with the sensitivity of a gnat wrapped in foil which I can use to test the circuit. The logic goes that a short circuit will result in a current to flow to earth, however the RCD will automatically switch off with a sensitivity measured in milliamps before anything nasty (like me becoming part of the circuit) can occur. One by one each circuit was wired into the builder's box. Only one errant nail in the loft blots my otherwise 100% copy book.

Getting connected
(or to which institution do you belong?)

If you thought the secret brotherhood of plumbers was daunting wait till you see what tangled webs are woven by those broken up by government sponsored deregulation. Ever heard the phrase "one stop shopping"? The late 90s equivalent was: "Guess which department has the remit to make decisions?" I'm reminded of those witches of Greek mythology who took it in turn to have the one seeing eye amongst them. You can almost see the internal emails within electric bureauland "would whoever has the corporate decision making widget please return it to the customer connections please" as some bugger (sorry, customer) wants us to make a decision. This particular conspiracy started long before we even cut the first piece of ground. Naively I thought I had the measure of the beast having spoken to a couple of sparkies and the local building regulations officer. The story goes something like...I know I'll ring up the electricity board to find out what they need to be in place and tested before making us live. "Hello I'm building a house and need to establish the rules with regard to converting my builder's box to a live domestic supply, please", pause "sorry, which company are you from"? "Myself, I'm a selfbuilder, I'm planning to wire the house myself to the eye triple E guidelines and need to know what testing you would need conducted". Pause. "So you work for the eye triple eee". "Nooo, do you have a department that connects up new premises?". "Yes it's a freephone number 0800 666 666". Eventually you get a bloke on his tea break, between dipping his rich tea biscuits it emerges that they actually don't give a monkey's who does the work or the testing "cos if it don't pass our test on the day we'll be charging you for the next visit". Sounds like the Mafia with multimeters doesn't it? Nice. A little glimmer in the cloud came from Jenny in Building Control.

Apparently the building control people were becoming aware of the confusion and were putting together a mandate that meant that a professional trade association member would need to test any new installations as part of the regs. Sign off. I really do not know how far they got with this but the next can of worms beckoned. Trade organisations just love TLAs (three letter acronyms to you and me) or better still four letter ones. So out came the yellow pages and a quick scan of the trade organisations page. There's something distinct in the British psyche about all agreeing to do things the same way, i.e. we don't . Island mentality, maybe, but mention the word standardisation and we kick up our tresses and start our own special way of doing things. At best it leads to creativity from chaos, at worse frustration amongst the end users. In IT we had this down to a fine art, but these buggers have me awestruck, I'm simply not worthy. Here's some letters. IEEE – the main institute for all things electrical in the UK. They wrote the book of how and what and have more revisions to the book than Delia Smith on amphetamines. Then there is the ECA who at the time of writing were in dispute with the IEEE over god knows what.

My main concern beyond getting certified is the earth continuity requirements. Since I'm using plastic plumbing in most places do I actually need earth cables linking porcelain and plastic in the bathroom? So I threw another acronym into the pot. OFTEC, these are the oil heating guys and at last I get confirmation that the pipework in and around the boiler does indeed need earthing. Great! As for the rest now I'm getting contradictory advice: one lot want me to dig holes in the plaster and run in some (as it turns out redundant earthing) to everything, just in case. The other (you guess which one) is considering the implications of this new fangled plastic plumbing on the trade. That would be the stuff that has been in circulation for about three years then would it? All I want is someone to check my work and ensure that when the board does turn up it will all be okay, the birds will sing and the fridge will hum contentedly into life after three years in a garage. I need help and I find him on a postcard in the local shop. He has a B.Sc. Hons and IEEE certification to his name so even if he is in the wrong band politically at least he has the inside track on getting a look at the bible (i.e. the Regs, cue angelic chorus). He is also a local man and closely resembles that nutter on TV who chases poisonous snakes around the world. But is he up to making sense of my well meaning but essentially amateur efforts?

The snake chaser turned up the next day wearing suede desert boots and carrying a rucksack full of widgets. Next, he proceeded to walk around the abode asking questions as he went. I decide this is a bit too much like those moments that you spend in a MOT waiting room anticipating big expenditure so I departed stage left. Two hours on and the post mortem begins. Things aren't too bad at all. One bad connection in the cooker outlet and some tidying up of cable sleeving in the attic is all that is needed. I'm elated and the follow up letter confirming the schedule of works hints at praise for my efforts. Maybe I'll set up my own professional body after all. The return visit sees a clean bill of health and the coveted partial certification (they can only give full certification if they did the work as well). Now I'm ready to take on the board. "Bring on the testers," I challenge down the phone. And they did. The men from the board bring a combination of both what I used (plug in tester) and what my man used and declare all is well. Connect me up, Scotty. This is a tense moment; the switch is thrown and we wait expectantly. Nothing happens, which is good. Next I close in on the consumer box and throw all the switches on. Again quiet. First the lights, check. Then the sockets, check. Then the big one ten amps worth of current down the line to the cooker. Whooeee we're (a)live.

At this point I went on a lap of glory around the garden punching the air. Grandpa Walton and his mates don't turn an hair which is sad since they have obviously got used to demented ravings from over here. At the end of the day the smile on my face wasn't from too many electric shocks but from achieving something I only knew a smidgen about at the start and in triumph over bureaucracy's best efforts to thwart me. A quiet doff of the cap to Obi Wan and a glass of vino closes the day off nicely.

On the home front, ultrasound scans are the order of the day. As we huddled around the monitor to get a first glimpse of junior we're delighted it's a healthy sprog. It is also a boy and he seems to be holding a cordless drill in his hands smiling back at us. That'll be handy I mused at the time, he likes tools (how prophetic that turned out to be)! Back at the ranch, however, babies aren't the only thing expected. Around these parts there's an unwritten rule which goes: "when they cut the corn and evict the wildlife they punish us by coming to live in our homes". I guess that is a bit like moving back in with your parents after you left home. Anyway, true to form as the combine harvester did its worst so did they.

There's something really attractive to the rural rat about housing developments. Maybe it's fact that you haven't had a chance to hermetically seal every orifice yet. Or perhaps that freshly laid plasterboard in the loft means they don't have to practice balancing along beams anymore. We compounded the problem by firstly having a pet rabbit in the backyard and secondly by leaving a gap near the stable door unblocked. One morning after a fitful night's sleep listening to the buggers tap dance in the attic space all night I was jabbed in the ribs by the small whale lying next to me. "They're in the house" she said. So up I jumped brave but bare and cautiously looked down the corridor. Last night's fish and chips was jigging about in the refuse sack and without a moment's hesitation I picked up a piece of plasterboard and started beating the bag into submission. I'll never know whether it was the sight of my naked body or the beating which made the beast leap up and away down the offending gap. Which as you might imagine was rapidly sealed.

The next morning I called in the council rat man. You know that thing about dog owners and their pets looking alike? This was him, the rat man of old Cambridge complete with threadbare whiskers (sorry beard). I fully expected him to have pelts hanging from his belt, Davey Crocket fashion, but no, he has the goods and a grudging respect for the enemy. Over a coffee we discussed the horror stories of cornered rats going for the neck. Nope, popular fiction. Rats will aim for the light, which when they're cornered is usually over your shoulder. So we walked around the building and quickly realise that we might as well advertise in the *Rat Times* so open and inviting is our "pied-à terre". Unfortunately, word was out on the streets and we had Ratty Adams back several times before they stopped treating our home as their winter residence. This type of invasion is more common than you think and treated like some kind of social leprosy. That is until most of the street had little visitors of their own. Rats are, by common agreement, clever and difficult to get rid of. Even we had a grudging respect for the way they eluded our attempts to keep them out. One little rascal used to dart out from underneath a plank, sprint to the rabbit pen mission impossible style, squeeze through the netting and help himself to bunny's crumbs.

Keeping cats won't do much other than keep you in dead carcasses from time to time. Even my mate's Jack Russell took one look at the attic space and turned tail. Like children, rats won't even eat their food when you want them to. So the best advice is be aware of what attracts them in the first place. It's food. Our bunny without knowing it sent a signal of comfortable living across the fields. Once in proximity any access big enough (and it's smaller than you think) will be explored. Just knowing they were there played all sorts of tricks with my head when trying to sleep. At one point I thought seriously about laying a grid of chicken wire across the whole attic space. Then with about 240 volts linked in we could toast and sleep well into the night. Enough of this, it's making me itch!

So the advice is to make sure that the drain access and ventilation holes are soundly blocked. Further, try and locate any sources of food well away from the house. We moved the rabbit and the following week a young vixen popped in for a take away. The rabbit stamped his feet and did some karate and so lived to tell the tale. But that's another story. Time to get back to the plot.

Second fix plumbing
(or down to brass taps)

One of the nicer surprises of this lark is when a product vendor provides assistance beyond the call of duty. Maybe it's just good business practice by one or two enlightened companies. Whatever prompts it, I am happy to recommend the event to others in similar states of confusion. This one concerns the way that all the waste pipes fit together both under and above ground and the roll of honour names OSMA (or Wavin products) to step up to the stage.

Many moons back I hooked up with the technical support department of the company and was delighted to receive by return a complete (detailed) schematic of every single piece of pipe and connector required for the build. This went from the initial brown (110mm) waste pipes running to the main sewer spur all the way up to the connecting widgets for the sinks and water closets.

In fact, if you ever enjoyed playing with Meccano as a child this very probably is a dream come true. We had literally dozens of large plastic bags turn up, along with the master plan. The hardest part was locating the numbers on the side of the individual parts, with one exception. The schematic says I should have a 110mm spigot reducing connector linking to a ninety degree bend offset before disappearing down the waste pipe. Whooeee, after this I'm ready for Apollo 11.

Fortunately, the Cavalry was on standby and the local sales rep came out to shed some light on things. I guess the lesson here is to contact the vendors directly prior to ordering and ask what help they are willing and able to offer. I really cannot imagine what the degree of assistance I received was worth in hard cash.

However, I do remember the feeling of elation when the wc hooked up and we had the portable loo towed away. If you have done your homework with regard to how and where the sanitaryware is fixed then the next step should run smoothly. After many months of fighting the subbies for first dibs in the site toilet our own flushing loo was the ultimate luxury. Likewise with that first hot bath. But first we had to get a hot water supply in place.

Nemesis the boiler

The moment has arrived and we are eye to eye gauging each other for signs of weakness. Standing one and half metres high with a cubic capacity to scare a hot rod the combined bulk of my boiler and Energy Master cylinder presents a formidable sight. I've been avoiding this part of the game for a long time. My approach is well considered and researched to the teeth. Of all the things that needed doing either by myself or someone more knowledgeable, the process of installing the heating system is the one that scares me the most. It's not just the blatant unhelpfulness of the plumbing trade as a whole that bothers me since I found ways around that particular hurdle by going to the manufacturers directly and banging on their doors until I got the lore I needed for the job. No this is about the consequences of making mistakes. It's about turning all that mains water loose within the system. It's about where electrics, oil and water all meet. More importantly, it's about whether the missus gets to have her first tap powered hot bath!

So to the cast. In the blue corner, 60,000BTUs worth of pristine oil-fired boiler. In the red corner, one proprietary hot water storage device (NuHeat). Scattered about the floor sundry manifolds, valves, computer chip driven thermostats and several miles of underfloor heating tubing. In the middle, several installation manuals, towels, mops and buckets just in case, and yours truly. As ever, I've read and re-read all the instructions and laid all the bits out in the order they'll be needed. By the letter it starts with some planning.

The basic premise of water powered underfloor heating is that mains water pressure drives the whole thing, thus avoiding the need for a couple of coffins in the attic space. Central to this is a big insulated cylinder which acts as a heat reservoir. The heat is provided via a closed loop from the flow and return outlets in the boiler. This then heats a jacket of water in the body of the Energy Master cylinder. Hot water for baths etc is drawn from the top (where it's hottest) and the cooler water from the bottom serves the underfloor heating.

All the above is then controlled by a network of thermostats and a central computer chip. Sounds simple doesn't it? Well fundamentally it is. Once you have your mind around how the whole thing hangs together and you are reasonably happy with reading schematics (electrical and plumbing) it all makes sense. That's because I've done it and can afford to sound smug. We bought our system from NuHeat and the boiler from Firebird (whom they recommended). The manual gave a step by step guide including a CAD designed installation specific to our home. Before starting I worked out exactly where all the flow and return pipework would go – right down to the holes in the ceiling.

The schedule of works goes something like:

1. Lay DPM onto block and beam floor.
2. Cut and lay 50mm polystyrene insulation over the DPM.
3. Lay out the tubing which carries the hot water to a set design.
4. Inflate to pre-determined pressure and check for leaks.
5. Connect all controlling manifolds and box in to protect from screed.
6. Lay screed.
7. Install boiler and cylinder
8. Complete electrical work.
9. Test and commission.

First fixing meant that any pipework that needed to be hidden behind plaster has to be labelled (using the trusty coloured tape, red for hot etc). My particular installation is above a block and beam suspended floor. Onto this I have laid a high gauge damp proof membrane and SDM expanded polystyrene insulation sheets. The actual heating tubes will then lay on top with a strong mix of screed laid over the whole thing. Which after the block and beam floor is something I didn't plan to do myself!

I do however have ten tonnes of sharp sand sitting on the front drive to remind me about this particular critical path.

Putting down the DPM and insulation was a pleasant job not only because it doesn't take long to do, but also because you get to see the fruits of your labours immediately (which is rare in this game).

More importantly playing with giant pieces of polystyrene reminds you of your childhood. Next up the tubing. Mandy really went for this one big time and it is fair to say she did the majority of the work. In the early stages of the self build so much work involves physical labouring that there wasn't a lot she was able to do. Sometimes this became a bit frustrating since this is a joint effort. So this opportunity to get her hands dirty was a welcome break for both of us. Miles of red pipework laid to a precise plan duly inflated and pressurised and we are ready to call in the screeder. Finding a screeder was one of the more difficult skills to pin down since it lies between the premises of both a plasterer and general building contractor. I interviewed three in total. The first bloke walked in chewing gum, pulled a figure out of the air and made it known that he'd prefer weekends, cash and yours truly to act as his labouring boy. Well that wasn't the plan and I smiled politely as I showed him the door.

Second man on site was a local Herbert who'd heard down the pub that some geezer up the hill needed a floor putting down. Had he ever laid screed over underfloor heating I enquired. He hadn't and to be quite honest wasn't sure about the right mix required, but he would ask his mate who knew about such things. Hmmmm!

When Steve turned up complete with tape measure, a calculator and a diary I felt hopeful for the first time. What was more he knew the exact mix required, had just come hot from a Potton development up the road (so knew his potatoes about timber frames) and could start in a couple of weeks time. Which, as it happened, was when we anticipated finishing the pipes.

To the sound of Mandy being thrashed to meet the deadline we anticipated the raising of the floor level.

Wheelbarrows on fire

Now there are people that work hard and there are grafters. Then there's Steve and his brother-in-law.

Second fixing – down to brass taps

Whether it was the incentive of a fixed price job or that the boys were on steroids I never knew. But pound for pound I could probably build a small estate with this combo. Having never seen sparks coming off a wheelbarrow before it's not just me who's impressed; Grandpa Walton takes notes and a phone number. It took about three days to move ten tonnes of sand and a pallet load of Portland's finest cement into and onto the floor. The mixer is panting and the wheelbarrow is waving a white flag but by golly we now have a finished floor level – all 65mm of it.

By comparison the second fix plumbing is a sedate quiet time only punctuated by yelps of whoopee as warm water flows into virgin sanitary ware. This is the moment when the time spent getting the exact measurements for fixing points for the noggings pays dividends. Likewise, all that pipework sticking out of the walls suddenly makes sense. See there was some kind of logic to this! Not for the first time I am eternally grateful to John Guest for putting his name to a particular brand of plastic pipework as I merrily snip and snap connectors into place. Since we've had running water of a fashion for some time (i.e. a hose pipe attached to the side of the bathroom sink) the advent of a plumbed in WC doesn't really excite.

The biggest thrill for me is the moment I turn on all the bits and bobs for the heating system and watch as the boiler fires up (OFTEC commissioned first) and presents our first hot water bath. So is a hot bath better than sex? After months of living in grime and clogging up other peoples pipes you better believe it is! Sad, I know.

Second fix carpentry
(what it's like to build your own kitchen)

I have a perverse nature. Maybe it's prerequisite to becoming a selfbuilder. I have this innate belief that with enough time, study and help I can do most things. This is akin to that chaos theory that states that a typewriter and an infinite number of monkeys and time would lead to the complete works of Shakespeare being produced.

Sadly, I'm the only monkey and it's my wife who now hangs from trees gibbering. Before we even thought about building my rallying call on any task that looked overpriced and within the wit of this mortal man would be "I could do that". This time maybe I went too far.

You see I built the kitchen as well. Not from a kit, not from a stack of pre-assembled bits of laminated MDF. I built the whole flipping thing from the ground upwards! So hence the title to this section. At the start we both looked at which big expenses we could have some control over. Excluding anything structural, this came down to the sanitaryware and kitchen. Well even I know my limitations in casting ceramics so the toilet was safe.

However, as a long time dabbler in all things wooden, I just knew I could muster up something myself in the kitchen area.Which I did. Slowly. In fact, of all the jobs around this house this one took the longest time and involved the most fiddling. In fact, I am still tinkering as we go to print! I'll spare you the details since they are well documented in a well known self build magazine a few years back.

However, I would share some pearls of wisdom with you just in case you are contemplating doing it. DON'T. The reason that kitchens seem expensive is because there are loads of fiddly tricks of the trade and specialist tools for creating all the mouldings. Granted, it can't cost much for a manufacturer to knock out set designs around a common template. But for Joe Average with a circular saw and a router to his or her name it's a lot of messing about. That's the down side, here's the up.

I built my kitchen for about £1,000. Compared to quotations back in 1999 of between £5,500 and £7,000 for our heart's desire, that's a big saving. Since that time, prices have come tumbling down which is good news for all.

We also have a completely unique, "nobody in the whole world has a kitchen like this" design which has literally been hand-crafted from raw materials. I kept my purchases of specialist tools down to things I could use elsewhere such as a truly excellent cross cut/ripsaw combination bench from Triton, plus a biscuit jointing outfit.

At the peak, I had 16 sheets of 8ft x4ft melamine faced chipboard (MFC) sitting in the garage. At the end of it all my arms are three inches longer, I swagger like an Orang-utan and I have a new found respect for kitchen manufacturers.

Given the dosh, I wouldn't do it again and that's the bottom line – we didn't have the dosh so we had to. For those of you so inclined here are some tips:–

* Start by drafting a layout on top of a copy of your building regs. drawings. Take these along to one of the weekend DIY megastores as a starting point then choose a couple of design themes that are both relatively simple and aesthetically pleasing (i.e. you like them).
* Within the design try to focus on the main theme, for example we have an arched look across all the door tops and interior features of our kitchen. Next, examine how that look can be duplicated using the skills and equipment you have available to you.
* Crunch time is when you decide on the trade-off between how much you make versus how much prefabricated bought in material is used. There's a logical split between the carcassing work (i.e. the cupboards) and the doors. Either of these can be bought independently and fitted depending on which bit you choose to do.
* Have a good hard look at how adept you are with a spindle moulder (router plus fixed table) and circular saw. Since this is a highly visible aspect of your home can you afford to take chances?
* Check with your local builders merchants about the availability of materials and delivery. Remember that whilst buying bulk costs less (proportionally) multiple sheets of MFC weigh a tonne, take up a lot of space and require the dexterity of a JCB operator to manipulate.
* If you are still determined to go ahead try to get hold of the back issues of *SelfBuild&Design* Magazine where I go into a lot more detail. Good luck.

Second fix childbirth

At the end of this phase the world suddenly turned upside down. It's not that I'm no good at project management. Quite the reverse, in fact. No it's when your tasks get inexplicably completed earlier, which up to this point had never happened. Mandy gave birth about six weeks early and everything just stopped. Well, not everything. For a start, when the waters broke instead of asking for a stopcock she just casually mentioned it on the way to the overnight bag. I suppose after more than a few years of non-conventional living this was just something else to deal with. So I covered the car seats with a DPM (see how sensitive we blokes can be) and set off down the M11. Nineteen hours later Connor John Self Build Gray was born and, as all parents will tell you, life will never be the same again. For a start, I'm now doubling up as night nurse. Holding babe, I quickly mastered the art of house building one handed whilst doing something else with self tapping screws. Like living next to a black hole, time gets distorted and slows down. At this point we called in the Cavalry. Every friend and family member we could think of was invited around to help (sounds better that way doesn't it)? Suddenly walls got painted, ceilings got Artexed and loose ends began (at least) to get tied up. Why didn't we think of this before? Pride, I think. Pride hasn't really got a place when you're tired and worn out by the whole thing and haven't the funds to hire in extra help. Our mates rallied and rallied big time in a way that we will never be able to repay them. Their names are at the front of this book.

I think that it is fair to say that the self build project went on hold for about the next six months. Whilst Mandy took maternity leave from May to August I dabbled with the kitchen and put up a few shelves. Come August, however, my career took another twist and I ended up as a full time house dad. Nowadays, there seems to be a lot more blokes staying at home and this I applaud. If nothing else this little role reversal gives both parties an insight as to how it feels to wear the trousers (or pantyhose in my case). This was also another of those moments that I describe in Chapter 8 as giving your relationship a belt with the angle grinder. On the whole I enjoyed those early months and took special joy in scaring the pants off the local mother and toddlers club with my presence. But, and it's a big but, the house build was glaring at me to finish the job. Between feeds and nappy changes I would sprint around the house trying to cram in odd bits of work. As any parent at home charged with child care will tell you, it doesn't work. So at about five months old we put our little soldier into a nursery for two days a week. Apart from the obvious trauma of separation and the little twitch he developed, it didn't do him any harm. Better still, I was back on the job. But I needed some help now to try and get this beast back on the road, starting with the carpentry.

"I don't mind you blokes having a go, but you see I'm a professional"

I thought about doors for a long time and had this nagging suspicion that it looked a lot easier than was in fact the case. As it happened, time and the wife's boney waggling digit carried the day. So I employed a local bloke who used to do exactly this for a living before throwing it all in for a reliable job in the local supermarket warehouse. The trouble was that one of those wooden chips flying around in his past life had settled on his shoulder. We're about to hear some immortal lines starting with : "Now I don't mind you blokes having a go, but you see I'm a professional", and he has all the tools to prove it. Ironically, it's this 'time to do the job plus having the tools argument' that I preach so often in my writings that has finally caught me up. I'm still messing around in the kitchen and do not have six hundred quid's worth of Radial arm saw at my immediate disposal. Nor do I have 25 years plus of distilled tricks of the trade to whip out at a moment's notice.

Ego aside (which isn't easy since there's barely room in the corridor for all of us) the man knows his potatoes and the linings start to move into place. Great, I think, I'll just get on. Big mistake. "Sooo you built this kitchen yourself did you"? I have the male equivalent of someone running their fingers along the edge looking for dust, in my kitchen looking over (what seems like) my lifetime's work.

"Biscuit jointed it did you? Yes, that's okay if you don't need a strong joint, I guess". I'm waiting for the "in my day" speech with clenched teeth and a chisel. "Well," say I, "how long have you been out the trade?" getting into the swing of it (all that coaching with the mother-in-law is coming in useful). "Technology has moved on quite a bit now, this is faster and I guess cheaper than paying someone to cut hundreds of little mortise joints". Fifteen all. But we're not done yet. Some minutes on.

"You did know that the frame isn't square didn't you?" Thirty fifteen. "Because I'm having a hell of a job getting these linings in straight. Forty fifteen. "Well do your best mate, it'll probably take a few to get your eye back after so long out of the game". Forty thirty. "Are you managing, do you want me to give you a hand?". Duece and new balls – his, if this carries on. Before we go to Advantage I call time out and make tea. Then I notice that it's six o'clock and time for Star Trek. I might as well concede the whole match now since being a Trekkie is the final confirmation from the man.

"So what's so good about a load of blokes who don't exist doing things they never could do in real life then"? Dunks biscuit, smiles. "Imagination, my friend, good for the soul", breaks racquet, reaches for the video recorder. It's going to be a long, long evening.

Nine doors and their linings on we've got him back to tackle the architraves and skirtings. By now I know the game and keep a low profile and away from anything that threatens to encroach on the sacred turf of carpentry. The irony is that whilst there are some short cuts to hanging doors it isn't rocket science. Mostly it's about getting everything square and the application of wedges. Chippies come in two flavours – building site oppo's and cabinet makers. The former focus on the whack, bash and cut school of thought whilst the latter are more leisurely and crafts focused and can make a timber joint into a piece of art. Many can and will do both aspects. However, the demand is mostly for blokes handy with a tape measure, a hammer and a throw away saw. This double aspect to a tradesman's skill is something I've seen a lot of since starting. My bricklayer's eyes moistened over at the prospect of helping with the design of our fireplace before finally building it. The Artexers let it be known that the more arty the finish the happier they'd be. I guess there are only so many swirl patterns you can stomach! Meanwhile, we've reached an impasse in the architrave fixing department.

For my sins I have invested in a trade pack of No more Nails tube mastic things, the claim of which is just that. It was always my aim to steer clear of the need to back fill recessed nail holes by using these products. The ego with the saw, however, has other ideas and holds up an ever so slightly warped length of timber as exhibit A.

The problem is that when you engage a tradesman, by implication you endorse (within reason) their method of working. Can I be bothered for a rematch? I look around the edges at all the non-standard internal angles we have built into the house and decide not. Nails and bludgeons carry the day.

The lesson to be learned? Make your thoughts about non-standard approaches to construction known up front. My mistake was to assume that the latest technology might make its way into established thinking. I've been here before with the plumbing so I mark this one down to a lesson re-learned. The other part of the equation is, just how bothered about it are you? I outsourced the job in the first place as I didn't have the time to mess around so letting the man get on despite a minor cosmetic issue kept the work moving forward. By the end of a couple of days of chest beating and bitching we have doors and a new found privacy missing for about 18 months. Will I miss the plywood hanging on stable hinges ? No, I think not.

Finishing touches

Getting towards the end of the build a young man's (or woman's) fancy turns to the more cosmetic aspects of the build. Unfortunately, at this stage the chances are that fatigue and just plain apathy are starting to take their toll. Fear not, most experienced selfbuilders (serial and repeat offenders) experience this at some (if not many) stages. One technique I employed repeatedly throughout the build was to make lists followed by an off-site summit meeting with the finance director (i.e. the wife). From this we then had to decide whether we can (a) afford to pay someone to do it; (b) do it ourselves; or (c) a bit of both. Avoid if you can making a sprint for the finish line and moving in (by which I mean full blown furniture stampede) ahead of schedule with the promise "we'll finish at our leisure" because you won't. Trust me on this! At this point in time even a bare screeded floor with rugs looked more tempting than waiting. Our 'to do' list comprised: plaster coving, Artexing and laminate flooring.

Even though unfashionable we opted for plaster coving throughout most of our abode. Once again there are a few tricks of the trade to bear in mind. The first is to use Artex itself as the adhesive. It has the same amount of grip, allows more movement when lining up and, better still, costs a lot less. When butting up pieces of coving do not cut the joints at ninety degrees as these are hard to disguise. First of all buy a 45 degree mitre guide which is a small triangular device which you rest the saw against when cutting. Avoid at all costs the cheap plastic ones the weekend DIY shops sell and opt instead for the professional metal one which won't bend out of shape as soon as you use it. This is then used to cut the angles for both the internal and external corners. Better still, use it to cut the butt joints since these are easier to hide in the finish. Finally, on coving you will inevitably have at least one piece which won't stick immediately. In these circumstances you will need to construct what the trade (I jest not) calls a "dead man". This is a "T" shaped length of wood (i.e. one straight with a cross member fixed at the top) which can be used to gently wedge or support the coving until it holds. We called ours "Buddy". Sad really!

Let's get one thing clear from the start. Artexing and textured paint finishes are not the same thing. Artexing is more akin to plastering and requires preparation, some creative ability and a lot of effort. Texture paints you buy ready mixed from B&Q, and require no more dexterity than the ability to use a roller unsupervised. So here was another job I undertook then allowed others (generously) to do it for me. To explain. I wanted to do all the Artexing and cracked on with both the study and bathrooms (my logic being they were small and less visible).

What I learned was that the real art in Artexing is firstly getting the mix right and secondly acknowledging that you need to trowel the flipping stuff on first. Hence the definition at the start of the paragraph. Yours truly tried to apply it with a textured roller first off which is akin to icing a cake with cement and a toothbrush! By the time we were ready to tackle our vaulted ceilings I bowed to spousal pressure to call in the professionals. Jez and Gary got recruited via a friend's recommendation and have been friends since school. Accordingly, they are more of a double act than Artexers. They're also really hard to pin down on account of being so busy which is always good testimony for a trade professional.

So they know their stuff and upon learning that I write for a well known magazine are happy to share knowledge for the promise of (maybe) a photo in the magazine. Which as it happened worked out nicely for all involved.

I have to say that whilst day one saw overalls and jeans by day two immaculate white overalls were in evidence with just a hint of hair gel. It gets better. They're star struck. Photo opportunities were never so frequent as I am summoned at every twist and turn of the proceedings. Artexing has never seen so much drama. However, they do know their stuff. So how should it be done?

Reading the instructions is a good start. The initial mix should be made using hot to tepid water to ensure that all the pockets of unmixed powder get beaten out. Using the appropriate mixer, always work down the sides of the bucket first to ensure complete mixing. Once the Artex has an even feel it needs to be 'knocked back' to a workable consistency by adding cold water. Professionals instinctively know by the feel when this point is reached. The manual suggests a point where the mixture just hangs in large drops off the end of the stirrer. A quick word on stirring/mixing devices. It is possible to buy or hire one attached to an industrial drill (do not even think about using your own tools on this). These are fine except at the point that the mix gets to a cement-like consistency and starts to spin the bucket around with it. Alternatively (but more work), use a manual metal mixer or a round piece of plywood with several one inch radius holes drilled attached to a long piece of wood. Before the main event all the visible and taped edges need an additional first coat of artex. This is known in the trade as 'caulking out' and its purpose is to hide any unsmooth surface features left by the taping process earlier.

Once you are ready to start choose one corner and work in one metre strips, adding the pattern as you go. To tidy up the edges and around lighting fixtures etc take a one inch wet brush and drag along whilst still wet. There are many possible patterns and it really is quite difficult to visualise how a sample design of a few inches will look once it's spread over many square metres. My approach was to pause after the first couple of patches had been completed and take stock. Since it takes a while to dry you have the chance to change your design (though not too often). It really is amazing what can be achieved using a sponge covered with a plastic carrier bag but that is exactly what it took for our designer old plaster look. You can paint it after a few days.

When it came to tackling the flooring our first consideration was the balance between our underfloor heating system's need to breath and the presence of a toddler hell bent on head butting the floor. Whilst we had always hankered after solid wood flooring we thought the risk of warping was too high. So the ever popular laminate wood effect flooring was chosen.

Since the whole thing floats as it were on a thin foam underlay we had the added advantage of a semi-sprung floor for junior. Buying the basic materials is pretty easy since everyone and his dog is selling it at discount these days. What I hadn't reckoned on was the astronomical cost of someone doing the work for you. Well there is nothing quite like a cash flow crisis to focus a selfbuilder's attention so I recruited a gullible friend and had a go myself. Here is what you will need:–

* A ruler and a decent tape.
* T-square or equivalent.
* Marker pen.
* Jigsaw with a few replacement blades or a couple of throwaway Tenon saws. The surface material is by necessity very tough and wears blades out rapidly.
* Plastic spacing blocks from the supplier, metal hook for tapping in "end grain" sections, tension straps, hammer.
* Laminate flooring (let them do the estimate and allow for wastage), glue, edging and underlay (2mm thick)
* Mitre block or saw combination (when fitting the edge finishers around and into corners).
* Cordless drill-driver (for attaching door grippers to the floor).
* Patience!

First read the instructions. Secondly, do the whole thing before fitting the skirting boards. It is possible to lay post second fix but a special edging needs to be fitted (which does not look so good). Having placed the underlay, start by building up (unglued) three to four sections along a straight wall using the plastic spacers. Next fiddle about until you are happy that both the fit is good and that the needs of expansion spaces are met (that is what the spacers are for). Dismantle and apply a thin layer

103

of adhesive in the groove of one side only and assemble using the tension straps across the boards and the metal hook down the lengths. I recommend using a spare piece of flooring to cushion your hammer blows on the hook/hammer tensioning. Otherwise the joints start to look a little mangled. Wipe excess adhesive away whilst still wet (it sets like concrete, be warned).

When cutting into tricky areas take a tip from tile fitters and turn the board upside down to cut the pattern in reverse underneath (this becomes more obvious when you do it). Alternatively, use a piece of cardboard as a template. It is fairly certain that some joints will look better than others. I used a clear wood glue with a dash of acrylic paint mixed in where the joints were wider than I hoped. The overall look is very impressive and lets the heat come through effectively.

In conclusion I guess we would all like to say that we did absolutely everything we could. The reality is sometimes getting in some help is just the tonic to speed up your occupation. Whether, like me, you were nagged into submission or common sense got to you first, remember you can always offer to hold the kettle whilst others do the (final) legwork, and then fib!

Chapter 8

Survival skills
(or, self build women are as tough as nails)

In my experience, whilst much is written about the logistics of building houses precious little is documented about the intangible other bits. You know, the bit about what to do when things go wrong (as they surely must) or when one of you wants either a hot bath by the weekend or a divorce by Tuesday (either will do)! After so many months of living in limbo there's so much to tell. But where to start? With the people involved, I think. Looking back, this took in a much broader spectrum of people than we could ever have guessed. So from we who went before, here are a few pointers so that maybe you'll have less grey hairs than I do now.

Primarily, there is your relationship with the wife, the lover, the partner, whomever you are undertaking this joint venture with. That really is the crux of it, the words 'joint' and 'shared'. If you are thinking about bearing this one all alone, think again. Even if you are single then those around whether they be friends or family will become surrogate wives and partners (though probably not lovers) when you need to let off steam because someone did not do what they were supposed to do on time or in the way you had expected. Perhaps I should call them co-dependants lending a touch of "self builders anonymous" to the proceedings. As we all stand up repeat after me "my name's Lez and I'm a selfbuilder". Better? So the first vote goes to them what shares the highs and the lows of this project. You know who you are!

From the very first moment that the hooks go in and the first addiction hits you, share it. After all this is probably going to a home for both of you in the foreseeable future and love's lost dream can quickly get bogged down in the footings as the first milestone comes and gets missed. To be honest, Mandy never really wanted to self build notably in light of all the chaos that was going on in our lives at the time. So lesson two is to gain commitment and do not above anything else railroad your dreams and aspirations down her or his throat. If your partner has concerns, and frankly if they do not then they are either naive or love you so much it's scary, then address them. One at a time with facts and logic not warm fluffy emotional platitudes. It is very easy at the beginning to fall in love with and get carried away with that Scandinavian love nest you saw in the brochure. Have you checked whether it is their dream too?

My wife and I almost routinely do not have the same ideas and views on what we both want. For some reason it seems to work better that way. Perhaps we both have contrary natures. What I do know is that it is a hard haul for one to convince the other that something is a good idea and sometimes it takes blood and pulled teeth to do i. The resultant acid test means that when we do agree on something it's been shaken to pieces for flaws. None more so than this little project. So compromise is the next lesson.

As the project moves along there will be highs as things progress and there will be lows as things seem to stagnate. In both instances talk about it. Get angry, rant and rave if you must but do not let it fester. Self building is a long haul and, as I say repeatedly, not for the faint-hearted. The lesson therefore is to communicate. This simple maxim extends well beyond the immediate range of partners. As a self builder what we do is considered odd by most, insane by many and perversely intriguing by the few. Thank god for the few! Of these, family members (we found) had the biggest problem understanding just why and what it was that drove us to give up sane living and all its comforts for an indeterminate period of time. Communication becomes more of a reassurance under these circumstances. I guess having watched the fledglings leave the nest only to start rearranging the twigs for themselves must be quite scary.

The process of self build also flushes out your true friends who, once over the shock of what you propose, will have a morbid fascination with progress. Our better friends offered not only sanctuary, hot baths, proper bed linen (i.e. not sleeping bags) and freshly cooked meals. A couple even offered pots of gold and hocked jewellery to keep the wolf from the door. Most of them even got press ganged into lending a hand from time to time. As ever, they know who they are. For our part a good bottle of wine and a take-away meal was usually all it took for us to relate the month's "tales from the caravan" saga. Choosing your friends by the size of their hot water tank is certainly a novel way of staying in touch! The survival lesson here is to accept with grace any offers of help from your friends and family. To say that self build sorts the wheat from the chaff does not even begin to do justice to what happens to your relationships, both old and new.

Moving on, with my foot very squarely in my mouth, are self build women as tough as masonry nails? I think they probably are. I also think that undertaking the build makes both parties aware of not only what made them feel like screaming but also how strong they both can be. Self build does not so much stretch your relationship as give it a belt with an angle grinder. But like forged steel, if it survives then it will be stronger. It also helps early on to identify what comforts you miss the most. We lived in a ten foot impoverished caravan for several months and the thing the missus missed the most was hot running water and the ability to have a soak in a deep deep bath. Well, the provision of mains water could not be rushed ahead of schedule but the siting of a bath could. I think it took about twenty or thirty electric kettles worth to fill that bath but the smile on the face and the back rub it secured more than made it worth while! On the other hand what I missed was simply space. Once I had more than one room to prowl around in and better still somewhere to let my hi-fi speakers breathe, life didn't seem so bad.

The next lesson is take time out for yourselves and play. Getting off site once a week, even if it's just a trip to the local supermarket, will remind you that there is life outside the building site and, better still, people not involved in the building trade. Our local swimming pool not only provided us with cheap showers but rest and recreation, and access to coffee making facilities!

Patience is not only a virtue but something you have to buy into early to stay sane. Ahead of you are months, possibly years, of living out of boxes or in someone else's abode. We often felt like we had put our lives on hold with all our favourite toys packed out of sight. Likewise, keeping a focus on the end product is a key to this game. Nothing ever happens as quickly as you hope and every now and again frustration at a perceived lack of progress will sneak up on you. These are the days when nothing goes right. You get fed up living in the mess and since a large part of the job of house building is in non-cosmetic stuff hidden behind walls progress never seems to be made.

On these days the trick is to firstly recognise them for what they are, grit your teeth and do something that delivers an immediate impact (like painting a wall). The more tangible this is the better. The next day things invariably don't look so bad. The other suggestion is one of discipline. Make a list of things you can achieve in a day and fastidiously stick to it. This one always works for me even if it starts with the day's washing up!

Where do you live during the build? I need to take a big breath here before committing words to paper probably in uppercase bold. You remember the bit about relationships and angle grinders? Well this was it. If we had camels and straws on backs they had my name on them. We lived in a second hand ten foot caravan with an awning. In the beginning this qualifies as romantic, novel, cosy even. Perfect if you are both four foot tall, weigh no more than six stone and enjoy secreting all your clothes into tiny little holes in the wall.

As it happens, I crack six three at 13 and a half stone. To state my wife's dimensions would be to invite bodily harm. Suffice to say although of sylph-like dimensions she certainly isn't a hobbit. Cramped and damp is not a recipe for long term harmony and I urge any acolyte self builders to pay due attention to all things domestic long before the first JCB hits site.

As a minimum I suggest :

* Hot water either in a bath or shower facility.
* Electric hook up – to plug into the builder's box if required.
* Cold water – ideally hooked to the stand pipe or as pumped resource via a large container if not.
* Heating – we had a built-in gas heater which could be left on all night. We also blew up two electric fan heaters with the damp!
* Space – be realistic about your needs not only to store clothes, food etc but also to prowl around and stretch your legs.
* TV/Radio – trust me you'll need some other form of diversion at the end of the day!
* Fridge/cooler box – for dairy products, of course (not beer).
* If possible a separate sleeping area that does not need putting away in the morning.

109

I guess the ideal scenario is either a portahome or to rent something nearby. Our budget would not support renting and the plot would not support anything larger than a 10-12ft caravan. We did, however, have some great barbecues! Having lived 50 miles from our last construction project we also learnt that it is desirable to be close to the build site due to security and the need for in-situ decision making. Getting towards the end as things begin to take shape, allow yourself to be a little smug. Not condescending but in a self-satisfied sort of way. After all, in the early stages there are plenty of less imaginative people queuing up to pour doubt on your undertakings. To these pour a large glass of something and toast yourselves for sticking at it.

There are few things in life as satisfying as designing and building a home around your personal needs. Maybe it's a primitive or instinctive thing but our homes reflect something of ourselves so a choice to make a stand against homogenised thinking has to be applauded. Cheers.

Hints:

1. Share the experience – both the highs and the lows (hopefully in equal measure).

2. Show commitment – this is a joint venture and sticking at it together and agreeing objectives with no surprises over individual expectations is paramount.

3. Compromise – if you plan to share your home with someone then some balance needs to be made between disparate expectations which are certain to be contentious.

4. Communicate – when things get tough, talk about it. Never ever let it fester or let the sun go down on unresolved issues. Self build is (more than) a little like going on a hike to the North Pole since you don't really know how hard it will be or how long it is going to take.

But whatever happens there is no escaping the person you started the journey with so you had better learn to start talking to each other.

5. Take comfort – recognise how important it is to pamper yourself from time to time and act upon it.

6. Play – Go off site, off subject (off licence?). Have fun!

7. Be patient – it's a long haul and you will get frustrated. Recognise the signs of frustration and apply the above. Then deal with it !

8. Focus – remember why you are doing this and what the future will look like.

9. Accommodate yourself sensibly – recognise the importance of where you live during the build and that it has to provide more than just somewhere to sleep.

10. Enjoy – when you do something well, enjoy the moment. Use it as a positive feeling to balance out the negatives along the way.

Chapter 9

Management Issues
(or it's my buck and I'll try if I want to)

This chapter looks at the often maligned, frequently misunderstood and, worst of all, poorly practised art of good project management, as applied to the joyous task of building your own home. No sane manager I have known ever claimed to be an expert and as one with the mental scars to prove it , neither do I. However, if we can take perverse pleasure in watching someone else make mistakes then we can equally learn from their pain. This chapter is dedicated therefore to all subbies and ex-team players who have suffered the benefit (good and bad times alike) of my leadership. I have deliberately broken this nebulous subject matter into seven sections in ascending level of importance:

* How much do you do; how much should they do ?
* So what does a project manager actually have to do ?
* Critical paths and how to avoid tripping over them.

* What was said was not what was heard.
* Let's talk about money.
* Man management and becoming an on-site
     agony aunt.
* Supplier management.
* Site management.
* Sundry shrewd and resourceful shenanigans!

How much do you do; how much should they do ?

There is a decision that needs to be made pretty early on in the build that affects not only the amount of money you have to spend but also your mental and physical health. If this sounds like an overly dramatic statement then good, it was meant that way. The decision you need to make before you even go shopping for funds is how much or how little involvement do you and/or your partner want in the project. Even the word project does not begin to describe what lies ahead – try 'campaign' or 'life-changing experience'. I can clearly remember the first day my brickie came on site and we began to get to know each other. Somewhere over lukewarm tea he predicted, quite accurately as it happens, that we would be different people at the end of the build. Well short of alien abductions I now know what he meant. On balance our relationship is stronger and our confidence in what we can achieve in life has grown many times. However, there was a lot of toil and emotional stress in there too.

In order to make a decision about your involvement you need to take a long hard look at your lifestyle and expectations. If, for example, the prospect of mucking in and spending virtually every free waking hour on the house appeals then do more. On the other hand, the ultra sensible yet no less valid way of doing things is to have someone manage the whole thing for you. I would suggest a sliding scale of complete hands off (i.e. what is known as outsourced project management) to up to your elbows in mud and plasterboard (i.e. doing most things). If the above scale goes from one to ten we kicked in at about eight. As a guide I suggest reviewing the following when making up your mind :-

1. Available funds – in all projects two types of money are identified, capital and revenue. Capital is the lump sum you actually have as tangible savings (hopefully earning interest somewhere). Available revenue is the difference between income from earnings (credit) and expenditure (debit) due to daily living. Without reiterating previous chapters it is suffice to say that the cost of building needs to be added to the cost of living. If you have enough money to employ someone to manage things then I suggest you allot a capital amount to that task rather than using revenue from earnings to pay for his or her time. Remember that capital actually exists whilst revenue only exist in the future and is only as stable as your means of making it.

2. Time – how much free time do you have right now? If you already conduct a frantic and busy social life are you prepared to give up some or all of that? How does the prospect of coming home after a day's toil to a pile of timber sound? Also ask yourself how long you are prepared to live in a temporary home with most of your possessions (and toys, even grown-ups need toys) in storage somewhere?

3. Children – I really could not write this chapter without this section. When we started we were two. When we ended we were four (baby plus ageing parent). There seem to be more and more stories appearing in self build magazines about self build parents who never got (family) planning permission when they started. Our excuse was the frequently lamented caravan and dodgy boxes of red wine!

On a serious note kids and self build can be both a nightmare and an exciting time in our lives. I simply implore you to take due account of the fact that both possibilities exist.

4. Skills – among virgin selfbuilders and the general public there is a view that building your own abode is akin to a bit of DIY fitted in at the weekend. The folly of this assumption becomes very clear, very early on. Being a bit handy with a Black and Decker does not a selfbuilder make. However, it is a start. There is a vast difference between banging up a couple of book shelves over a leisurely weekend and having to cut and nail 250 support noggings before the dryliner arrives first thing Monday morning. Since the aim of this book is to actually encourage rather than terrorise I offer the following advice based on the lessons we learned through both our successes and our mistakes. Be realistic in what you can do and what you would happily do on a much bigger scale. Conduct a risk analysis on each potential piece of work. (this is different to the site management risk analysis) and pose the following questions:

* Do I have the skill necessary to do this task competently?
* Am I confident that I can meet the deadlines required for the next trade on site to start their work or am I adding unnecessary delay to the project ?
* What is the implication to the project if I make a mistake? (i.e. in structural or cosmetic terms).
* What is the risk of personal injury?
* Would my time be better spent elsewhere (e.g. planning)?
* Will this task involve buying or hiring specialist tools that a tradesman would already have?
* The building game is physically demanding. Are you up to the task ? Tradesmen spend day in and day out lugging and lifting. Before I started building (although fit) my daily weight training was the teapot.

To bring this section to a close I would simply say this. Whether you choose to give the job of project management to someone else or take on the role yourself you will always ultimately be responsible for making things happen. If something (god forbid) happened to you whilst in the throes of wielding an unfamiliar piece of industrial grade machinery who carries on? Who will earn the money? Are you even covered on the insurance? Whilst it is true we did an awful lot of the work ourselves, I routinely avoided anything that involved structural components and warranties. Further, as a younger man I climbed rocks for a hobby. Did I undertake the roofing? No way Jose! Most people choose a compromise between hands on and project management. I chose (or was chosen) to do both. Looking back, had funds permitted I should have project managed only. This is a task for which I am well versed having spent about 15 years installing computer systems. So I swapped programmers for builders. Quite how this worked is detailed later in man management. The main point is that it is hard to keep changing hats mid-stream when a decision needs to be made.

To summarise, look at your personal circumstances very carefully and assess the risks and the benefits. A lot of satisfaction and saving can be gained from doing the work yourself but not, I suggest, at the cost of adding risk or delay to you or the project.

So what does a (self build) Project Manager have to do?

Whether you choose to manage or not it is important to at least know the fundamentals of good project management. That way, at least, you have a chance of recognising any cowboys before giving them a job on your ranch. Often a good one will charge a lot for their time and this adds a premium to the overall build budget. However, they should also save you both money and a few grey hairs in the long run.

So what skills should a project manager have? Planning? Yes, that is important. Financial acumen and accountancy skills are equally valid. Then what about the ability to grit teeth and stay focused when the brick company decides that you are too small a fish to worry about honouring agreed delivery times? Or listening to all your subbies' woes over lukewarm tea at 5 o'clock in the

116

morning? The simple truth is that project management requires such a broad range of seemingly incompatible skills that we might wonder whether such a divine being could exist. The bottom line is all of the above and more. If it is possible to simply lump the net task of delivering a completed house to the sponsors on time and within budget without loss of life or limb or mental capacity then that would be it. But it's not. The following section covers what I believe are the main components of good project management. The order in a loose ascendancy has the following logic to guide you. Foremost amongst project management skills is the need to put together a plan of works. In order to wield this plan effectively you need not only to be able to communicate your ideas but convince someone to give you their money. Once you have funding, the ability to control and monitor expenditure is paramount, along with the ability to motivate, lead and partake in whatever shenanigans it takes to get the job done. The last section of this part of the book is so named. The list is neither finite nor definitive, but since most of us learn something new on site every day, it is a good start.

Critical paths and how to avoid tripping over them!

Without sounding like an old record there is a maxim in business that goes "if you do not manage to plan, you do not plan to manage". This is the most important task of all and time should be set aside at least once a week to review progress. If possible obtain one of the project planning packages such as 'Project' (Microsoft) or PMW (Hoskyns) for your PC. In fact some of the newer computer aided design (CAD) packages on the market now routinely include basic planning software. Whatever you choose start by listing out the major tasks such as Groundworks, Services, Brickwork etc. You might even consider mind or bubble mapping on a blank piece of paper. This is an old technique (familiar to analysis and management consultants) whereby the first thought on the subject is written down in the middle of a blank piece of paper. For example this could be 'foundations' from which you might think of the word 'concrete' then maybe 'type of concrete'. Draw lines around these as bubbles and draw the lines to link them up. Very soon you will have fleshed out the main subject areas of the job in hand. It is then possible to see these as discrete pieces of work which can be lifted into a draft plan. It does not matter at this stage how complete or detailed they are since the whole process is iterative and the master plan will evolve with the project. View the project at two levels. The larger picture deals with the perceived (and trust me that is all it will be at the beginning) picture from start to finish, the Utopian just been to Alexandra Palace view of the world. The second level takes the particular most immediate task in hand and breaks it down into a do list. Things such as "must phone architect re: drawings" or "chase brick supplier ref. costings etc". These are details that would clog up the main plan but need doing at practical-keep-the-project-moving-forward level. I always kept a hardback A4 notebook with me, even on site (often covered in polythene). That way I always had any references (names, phone and invoice numbers) to hand as well as somewhere to note down any useful tit bits from the guys on site. Something you will quickly learn is to look for what are termed critical paths. These are tasks whose start or completion are dependant on other tasks. For example, the delivery of Readymix concrete (RMC) is dependant on having stable and open access to the trenches, what happens if the chute doesn't reach etc? Plan for the worst, hope for the best. For an example of a draft plan, see Appendix B.

What was said was not what was heard !

Professional communicators often cite the above phrase and this holds true in the building game as much as anywhere. Whilst it is not necessary (nor desirable) to be bosom pals with everyone on site the ability to talk to people makes life a lot easier. Fundamentally we need to be assured that our tradesmen have the necessary means to complete the job in hand as well as the focus to make it so. This comes down to obvious things such as sufficient materials and equipment (e.g. scaffolding) in place to planning ahead for linked or dependent tasks (see critical paths). However, no matter how often you stroll around the site (mugs of tea are always a welcome interruption) they will still catch you out. My brickie was constantly crying wolf over materials he didn't have enough of when all he wanted was someone to tell him what a great tradesman he was! You probably won't realise the need for this skill until it happens to you. In management speak, we used to call these reassuring pats on the back 'warm fluffies' and we all need them from time to time.

Think about it! How many of us spend hour after hour doing some mundane repetitive task without a single piece of feedback (good or bad) from our bosses? It is almost an acknowledgement that we exist if someone says "well done" from time to time. Building men might be as tough as toe tectors but they respond as much to flattery and hobnobs (biscuits to you and me) as their smooth-handed colleagues in offices.

My favourite case was a guy we got in to paint the garage woodwork. The ritual started with the daily briefing on what needed doing and in what order. We would both stroll around the site and I would point out things that needed special attention such as underneath the gable ends. Ten minutes on and the exact same words would be repeated back to me as if heard for the first time. My job was to enthusiastically agree with what was being suggested. He then had ownership of an idea I'd given him earlier.

The net result was we both had total buy-in with the boss's approval. All I have to do later is endorse what a good job he has done. The female readership out there will recognise this as a technique deployed upon us hapless menfolk since time began.

At some point in your research unfamiliar terms like purlins and lathe faced render start to creep into the game and this brings me to the noble art of industry jargon.

119

Every industry has its own jargon which has evolved out of the need to communicate ideas quickly and to keep outsiders in the dark. As an ex-IT manager I am as guilty as most on this score. In all probability, the first people you will chance upon will be sales staff maybe at the shows or via follow-up sessions on site. As I say repeatedly, if in doubt ask the question and compile your own glossary of terms, getting the salesmen to draw pictures if necessary. The golden rule is that there is no such thing as a stupid question since if you had to ask the question then it was not clear in the first place. Appendix A has my own list, compiled as I went along.

Let's talk about money

Here's the bottom line. Lose sight of cash flow and prepare to watch the project grind to a halt. The process of making and keeping a budget is a bit like painting the Severn Bridge. Better still, think of the process as a Zen thing whereby your first hesitant attempts are pretty inept but a start nonetheless. So you return and revise and refine, over and over again. Eventually, with so many refinements, the budget approaches financial Nirvana and enlightenment (or the VAT return). What I am trying to say is that the process of putting the budget together and the ongoing process of keeping on top of it are part of the same beast. I had been compiling forecast costings for at least a year before Building Regulations approval was received. I also read acres of background information on the whole thing with particular focus of costing the beast. Figures abounded as to how much per square foot one might expect depending on how much you did yourself. These ranged from as little as £28 to £45 or even £50 a square foot.

Here is my tip. Forget them. During the last four years building material prices went through the self build roof and of these aggregate prices have been the worst offender. There has been (and still is) a boom out there. Just look at the soaring price of building plots these days. Thankfully, the cost of spec-built homes has stayed sufficiently in front to still make this a good idea. My research took in information from a wide range of sources, ranging from the suppliers of self build homes, builders merchants, architects and local builders. A few even offered a quantities take-off service, based on the available information. All of these sources were analysed and comparative listings compiled. This particular exercise not only highlights the cost assumptions that suppliers make for their products, but also how much you know about construction specifics.

For example, do you know what grade and degree of slump is acceptable in your footings concrete? When you ring up for a quote you will certainly need to know before anyone will take you seriously enough to give you a quote! Like any industry a bare minimum of knowledge is required for entry into the inner sanctum. As small fish in the construction pond our pennies don't make much of a splash. So we need all the advantages we can get. Thankfully as your understanding grows two things happen. First, the communication among the main players becomes easier and, secondly, a more accurate picture of costs begins to appear because you actually understand what is involved. Then it's time to put together a working budget.

I was fortunate to have acquired a laptop computer from my old career and the accompanying software is still being put to good use. If you are not so blessed I recommend adding some pennies to your budget to acquire one. In fact, whoever invented the spreadsheet should be knighted for services to anyone who has ever had to collate financial information! Even the nice people the VAT office accept the returns in a spreadsheet format; why make life any harder? Within the spreadsheet I found the ability to create many layers of detail which was especially useful. These are usually called 'sheets' and the first one, the 'master', should have columns labelled for Gross, Net and VAT. Since the ultimate target (beyond building the house) is to retrieve a not insignificant amount of money back from HM Customs and Excise, make a point of getting hold of the special self build information package from their local office early on and look carefully at their format. After all, why duplicate effort at a later stage? Next, learn how to link specific cells to the front master sheet. In Lotus-123 this is the 'Edit, special link' option. I include an example in the Appendices as a guide. As information comes in from various sources, new sheets can be added starting with the preliminary costs such as legal expenses and surveys.

In addition to the build cost, potential financiers will want to know that you have given adequate thought to your current and future financial liabilities. So do not forget to set out your current financial position. You can often gloss over many things in life but the absolute never ever break rule concerns the money you have available for your self build. Lying to yourself will quickly lead to madness and a great deal of unnecessary additional stress.

Even if you recognise that the final finishing touches will have to wait or be downsized somewhat recognise the limitations up front, spit in its eye and move on. As a suggestion this is likely to cover:

* Salaries – Yours, your wife's, your children as chimney sweeps, whatever.

* Capital – all of your savings now and expected. This includes insurance policies, endowments (which will really give your age away if you have one of these), ISAs, TESSAs. Most importantly equity in your current property.

* Details of liabilities – debts, loans, direct debits etc.

* Basic living costs or assumptions – to include how and where you plan to live during the build. Do not forget to include travel costs if remote from the site or council tax liabilities if you live on site. This one really caught us out since we assumed that a 10ft decrepit caravan with precious little facilities and no completion certificate gave us immunity. But alas, no, the council enforcers sent

around spies and a nasty bill for £800 when we least expected nor could afford it.

So if you see any dubious looking people measuring up your temporary abode, you have been warned!

The final message is to return to the thought that budget management is an ongoing repetitive task which starts out very loose and vague. This then moves on to something you can use when approaching potential financiers, before finally arriving loaded with actual costings at the VAT returns office. At the point of presenting your efforts (in both cases), remember to set out your stall like a small business proposal (which of course it is), be professional and receptive to suggestions. Without doubt there is always the possibility of rejection. If so, learn from them and revise your approach accordingly. Banks and building society managers are by tradition cautious creatures. However some of them are a little more entrepreneurial and a sound proposal well thought out and presented will often make the difference.

Keeping on top of the budget

An important maxim is to start as you mean to go on. Initially this means getting yourself organised. Over the course of the build you will collect acres of paperwork and a small forest of delivery notes and invoices. This can easily get lost amongst the mud and clutter that will become your life. I invested in half a dozen box and lever arch files and collated information with a religious zeal. Come the day that the bills start coming in it's vital that delivery notes and invoices can be cross-referenced quickly and accurately. I always put aside one day a week for paperwork (usually Friday) to check and enter invoice details onto my trusty computer (which you should always, always back up). If possible, use the spreadsheet to detail forecast versus actual expenditure. Remember to make a copy of the first spreadsheet you construct at the time of getting funding and save this as the baseline budget for comparison later. Of particular importance is the cashflow prediction. List all known invoices and forecasts (gross of VAT because that is what is deducted from your funds not net) and their due dates to keep sight of the year-to-date (ytd) balance.

If you are plagued by staged payments then buying as many materials as possible through a builders merchants usually adds up to six weeks contingency, but do not get complacent. The closing thought in this section is to establish your construction priorities before you start building.

To explain, the absolutely-must-have works revolve around establishing the foundation and basic shell of the home. If things get tight moneywise, be prepared to delay or revise your immediate needs in the more cosmetic items. For us this meant buying more humble sanitaryware and looking around a bit more for finishing touches such as tiles etc that didn't have a designer label on them. Do not (like a recent example on TV) run out of funds before even the roof was put on (why did they even start?).

It is a well known joke amongst builders that self builders will skimp and scrape pennies on the basic fabric of the house only to blow the budget on a posh loo! After all you can always upgrade a toilet suite at a later date whereas roof tiles maybe not!

Man management and becoming an on-site agony aunt

We have this popular notion that blokes who work in the construction game must be tough as nails and live in trenches. Whilst one of the timber frame chippies did live in a chicken shack for a couple of nights it is easy to miss the point, which is that people respond to people, not building specifications or invoice notes. Something about shared adversity seems to open up communication channels especially on site. Only after the last man left our site did I stop feeling like an agony aunt. In total I feel like I've sat through three divorces, two extra maritals and a gaggle of personal mishaps along the way. One bloke proudly boasted of "giving one" to his accountant's missus whilst doing the end of year accounts. This is obviously some new form of double entry book keeping!

Another bloke not only played away from home but seemed to have a season ticket pre-booked on all the away games, plus no doubt a pre-season warm up. In total we met twitchers (bird watchers) with angst, a gaggle of messy divorces and at least one born again teenager. Through each of these we vicariously relived and survived to tell the story.

But what did we really learn? That preconceptions often get in the way of basic communication and that first impressions are just as likely to be in error as accurate. I met some extremely articulate and sharp individuals with whom topics ranging from the impact of the single European currency to matters philosophical were discussed. In fact I often found their company more stimulating than some of my degree wielding business acquaintances.

Many contractors are fairly nomadic in their quest for continuous employment and often spend many weeks at a time on the road. As one who has spent much time in nameless hotel rooms on business I can sympathise with this entirely. One evening we really did gather around a fire in the (early) garden and chew the fat with Chicken Shack Joe, the peripatetic New Age chippie. Over the course of numerous cans of beer I uncovered one of the sharpest brains I've ever met. Though in this case sadly dimmed by excess and child abuse. On a philosophical note this particular encounter brought our own discomfort sharply into focus.

The balance between listening to your subbies' woes and keeping the whip in plain sight is a difficult one. In the final analysis the calibre and timeliness of the works has to carry the day. Furthermore, although you are the boss and the source of your subbies' income for the next few weeks don't forget the human aspects of the project.

They might be as tough as marines but even the most hardened tradesman will respond to flattery, a hot cup of tea and a sympathetic ear to their domestic woes.

Finally, remember who is the boss. It is one thing having a great rapport with the blokes on site. And, yes, it is a wise man who seeks a more expert opinion on subjects new or alien to him(her).

But remember if things go wrong you need to be creditably firm and professional in your dealings. Gather together facts, check them, but at the end of the day it's your decision and your call.

Supplier management

You might find it a little arrogant to presume that suppliers can actually be manipulated in any way but as I used to say to one team I managed: "managers often need managing themselves by those they employ".
Furthermore, whilst I'm certainly no business guru I have found a few things that smooth the process of commerce. These are communication and consistency or in English say what you want and expect from a business relationship and be consistent in your dealings with people.

I'm going to say something quite unheard of here. I found a REALLY good salesman (from a builders merchants) who not only knew his potatoes about all things construction and played the rules of commerce fairly but I actually trusted and liked. Like most folk, I have known a few dodgy geezers in my time and somewhere amongst car salesmen and accountants there exists a warm boggy place in my heart for anyone (and I mean anyone) who tries to flog me something.

Kim comes from the Graham Group (before they were swallowed up by the Jewson Group) and he's a diamond and I wonder whether maybe I've spent too much time around BMW driving blokes called Nigel to cloud my judgement.

Anyway over the course of a few short years I've got used to him casually dropping in to check progress and see if I need a quote for anything.

Now this is really good practice since (i) he's always aware of the next likely materials I will need; (ii) I have quotes in well ahead of time; and (iii) anything I'm not clear about he knows someone who can help. Conversely, there's no bull. If he cannot compete on something he tells me up front which saves us both loads of (very precious) time.

There were a few less successful sales people along the way though. One bloke who claimed to be a plumber (oh good, I thought, expert help) promised the earth then changed jobs (and companies) in as many months. The spooky thing was that he kept on turning up in my patch all fresh and forgetful. I wondered at one point whether he simply wanted a coffee mug from each builders merchant for a collection. Who knows? Thankfully he disappeared myth-like into the ether along with half a dozen quote requests. Anyway, whomever you choose to do business with the universal language of trade is haggling and this warrants a section on its own.

In this country we polite British, keen not to offend, avoid the wondrous game of haggling. Elsewhere in the world it is viewed as part of the proceedings and not something over which civilised people take offence.

In fact, it could be argued that most grass root economies rely on the process to establish the true market value of commodities. Thankfully, things are changing and there is nothing quite like the focus of your house and ultimately your money being at stake to join in. Be warned though: knocking tens of pounds (or more) off the price of hundreds of facing bricks will only encourage you to try your hand in other markets. Before long you'll be haggling with the missus (or husband) over who does the washing up after a hard day's graft. You might even end up going to car boot sales (shock horror).

My advice is to approach the whole process with a smile and give it a go. To stand any chance of winning, however, you need to know what is happening out there. So at the beginning of the project always get a minimum of three quotes in writing (with an expiry date). Getting to know the business and what is being paid for what is one of the first skills you will need to acquire.

Likewise, letting the players know you are a serious punter with large chunks of cash to spend should get their attention.

Talk actual figures not blanket percentages and be straight talking, stating up front what you want and the quantities in question.

It is also useful if you have a modicum of knowledge about the products you seek to buy. A little knowledge went a long way on many occasions throughout my build. Imagine ringing up the supplier of ready mix concrete. "I'd like some concrete please". "Certainly sir, how many tonnes what slump and what grade?"

As it happened my soil survey gave me line and verse on RC35 with T16 bars throughout. Sounds good doesn't it? What this means is that you can compare products on a like for like basis and gain a little credibility with the tradespeople you deal with. Which is something you can't put a price on!

With a build budget measured in thousands of pounds you should expect the occasional expression of a merchant's gratitude for continued trade. My count's running at one two speed power drill, a 30 metre tape, T-shirts, wine, diaries and a site lamp (okay, I'm a tart)!

Site management and safety

With all the excitement in getting started on your new build it is easy to forget to give proper attention to the health and safety aspects of building. Selfbuilders more than big time spec builders need to be especially aware of the potential hazards in and around our new homes. From a statutory perspective the Health and Safety Executive (HSE) offered guidelines but precious little in the way of mandatory requirements prior to our build starting. Following an initial inquiry I was bombarded with all the HMSO publications I might purchase when all I really wanted was a checklist or audit of the pertinent safety issues.

The bottom line is to conduct a risk assessment and this falls to you the principle contractor (as you will be known) to conduct and manage accordingly. This should cover as a minimum the immediate physical environment, materials, service supplies, tools and their usage, first aid and insurance.

Clearly as the build goes on different risks arise but the simple task of walking around the building site and becoming familiar with the physical environment is a good place to start. Usually this starts with the access and entrances to the site. Our particular plot nestled amongst quiet village dwellings with a higher than average sprog population. Kids would not be kids if an inaccessible wilderness did not become magnetically appealing once opened. We were especially cautious since before a single brick was laid we had two very deep test pit holes excavated. Measuring one metre square and two metres deep, the rising spring line and thought of drowned offspring was enough for us to use a lot of boarding and fences to make it safe. Next, we recovered an old farm gate and liberally covered any excuse for an entrance with the red and white barrier tape available from builders merchants. Over zealous perhaps, but we next made known our plans and concerns to the neighbours before drowning their kids.

Moving around the site in both fair and foul weather (mostly foul) will highlight just how quickly conditions can change. Be aware of pits, puddles, ridges and hurdles. Use planks to bridge any bad bits and even consider throwing some sand into any particularly bad chasms! All of which should encourage you to practice good site management. From the start begin to identify areas where the different types of materials will be stored. Think about the access required and plan accordingly. If you leave the business of where to store materials to either the tradesman or delivery driver two things will happen.

The first is that your site will quickly become an obstacle course and you will constantly be moving materials from one place to another. The second involves cement sacks going hard before their time and timbers getting damp and mouldy. Get the idea? Part of your planning process should involve allocating spaces for your materials. This should include having sheets of polythene and, if possible, sacrificial pallet boards available to protect same.

One of the first materials on site will almost certainly be concrete and this presents its own set of safety concerns. Despite the mockery I received from the brickie's boy labourer, every time I moved a bag of cement I wore a face mask and gloves. This stuff is caustic and burns like hell if it gets on your skin and reacts with water. Think what it would do to your lungs! The bottom line is to read the instruction and warnings for all new chemicals brought on site.

The next job on site could well involve scaffolding and it is appropriate to stress the use of hard hats. I can testify to the sagacity of this practice. So can my head! You might even consider wrapping some sort of material around the pole ends.

Once the service trenches get dug make sure you know how to get out of them! Simple advice but valid is to leave a piece of timber or shovel in situ. This is placed across the trench and is used as a lever or step to get out!

Fortunately the electricity companies will only install power to a fully protected builder's box. Protection in this instance means a physical secure housing with RCD protection and a flipping great earth rod driven into the ground. My RCD was so sensitive that some of the heavier duty tools such as angle grinders kept tripping out. Sometimes irritating yet handy. I used this sensitivity to initially test all the internal wiring prior to a formal testing. Nevertheless a lot of your subbies will use 110V step down boxes which plug into the 240V supply for added safety. There is a colossal leap from a weekend DIY tool to the sort of heavy duty industrial tools you will buy-hire and see operated during your build. Becoming au fait with not only their use, but also awareness of their sheer destructive power is pre-requisite. If in doubt ask the supplier to show you the ropes. Often this will include safety issues not covered in the instruction manual as well as tips on best practice.

Bear in mind that most people can go and buy a chain saw off the shelf pretty much anywhere. I know a few people who work in woodland management and they are obliged to undertake extensive (and expensive) training in their use prior to even the most minor application. The other thought is, have you seen what an angle grinder can cut through? If you are in doubt, pay a professional to do it! Since it actually costs nothing to ask for advice be clear you are happy with any unfamiliar tools. I have a plumber friend who showed me how to solder copper pipe work and was glad of the tips on how not to set fire to the building!

With regard to protective clothing I recommend the following:

* Site hard hat for errant scaffold poles and over zealous brickies.

* Eye protection e.g. goggles or face shielding for sawdust, plasterboard dust, anything to do with glass fibre. Ballistic items(i.e. things that fly through the air) need special consideration.

* Face mask(s) – unless you are prepared to spend serious money on a full blown respirator the throw away type are best. Check with the supplier as to what type of particles the mask claims to filter. Be especially aware of any solvent based products that you use. The glue used to stick my above ground OSMA goods together went straight through the standard offerings. Keep windows open and ventilation active under these circumstances.

* Gloves – notably in dealing with fibreglass insulation. Also when materials threaten to cut, bruise or general maim your hands (e.g. blocks etc).

* Steel toed footwear (aka Toetectors) – a worthy investment up front. Do not, like a friend of mine, wear open toed sandals whilst moving sheets of chipboard. Not only will they protect your toes but the toughened soles will also deflect errant nails. It might also be an idea to check your tetanus status before you start.

   If an accident does occur on site you might want to ask yourself what First Aid you could effectively render. Thankfully, due to modern circuitry, an electric shock is pretty unlikely. However, cuts and breaks will always remain possibilities. I always carried an extensive first aid kit and made its location known to anyone I engaged on site. I also have a modicum of first aid and CPR training. Organisations such as St John Ambulance offer varying degrees of training and it might be worth checking these out. I also got a telephone line (albeit temporary) installed at the earliest opportunity in case I needed to call for help. Mobile phones are also worth considering? Although difficult for us keen selfbuilders try not to be the only person working on site at any one time. Likewise, do not leave anyone on their own!

On the subject of insurance be very clear about what cover you are getting for your money. The company underwriting the build (e.g. Zurich or NHBC) will have their own specific requirements for cover. Generally these come in two parts. The first covers the building as it gets built and should cover material theft and liability if it all falls down. The second part has to cover the liability for personal injury. Self build insurance is too complex a subject to cover here (not least of which because it is in constant change) so seek expert advice.

Remember, however, that when engaging subcontractors find out what insurance cover they have both for their own protection and due to works undertaken by them. Remember that not only do you have a responsibility to those who work for you but also as the principle resource on the project you owe it to yourself to avoid heroics.

The best safety equipment on site is your common sense. Respect both the build environment and the tools you use. Listen to the experts on site since the one certain thing they will not try to fib about (unless you are unlucky enough to employ a psychopath) are safety issues.

Sundry shrewd and resourceful tactics (or the art of scavenging)

Akin to the above is thinking about all those bits and pieces that nobody wants to pay for but keep the wheels of progress oiled. Things like wooden pegs for staking out profile boards, shuttering to contain aggregates and half cut scaffold planks to bridge muddy spots. I am by nature a magpie and pretty much everything left over from the build is stashed away somewhere with a view to its recycling and re-deployment.

The alternative, I guess, is to a have a skip permanently on turnaround which not only drains funds, impairs access but gives the non-magpie half of the relationship an easy route out. At worst, most hardcore can be used underneath patios or other garden landscaping. Most of timber used on our abode which had a nasty cocktail of preservatives within it could be used in garden features.

A word of warning, do not burn any preservative treated wood, not even in the great outdoors. The toxins are likely to include copper, arsenic and chromium, to name but a few. The local council dump should have a special place for their disposal if you cannot reuse their weather resistant properties elsewhere. The bottom line is hold on to (within reason) any structural material until the build is complete.

You would be amazed how many times I have reused planks and the concrete blocks from my suspended floor to bridge access points around the build. Likewise, the timber frame company left me several sacks of large galvanised ironware (at my request). The assorted joist hangers and nails now support the timber decking in my garden.

Juggling skills

Juggling such a multitude of skills isn't easy but with a little thought and determination more is possible than you might think. My golden rule in all things, whether I did them or not, was to research, research, research.

The other if not stranger rule I discovered was: when confronted with a seemingly insurmountable problem leave it alone for a while and come back to it later. Often when we go at a problem repeatably in our minds we inhibit the possibility of a solution finding its way into our consciousness.

I often found that either the answer became obvious or something happened to make it so the less I banged my head against the wall. Still deep, still building.

One final thought. To my knowledge there is no super hero called "Self Build Man". You will make mistakes, you cannot possibly know everything all we can do is our best. My secret weapon was to talk about the problems (or daily challenges) out loud to the missus. After all a problem shared. . . .

Chapter 10

How green is my chalet?

T hankfully the cry in the wilderness for a more sane
approach to building our future homes is much
louder than it was five years ago and subject to much
more public interest. Due in part, I suspect, to both media
interest and as a reaction to recent environmental disasters.
In fact it is now quite acceptable to talk openly in polite
company about a person's green credentials and I applaud
anything that puts the green debate in the public domain.
However, let's be honest. Before the floods and mad cows
anybody holding up their hand and suggesting there
might be a better way to do things was immediately
branded an idealist or card carrying hippie.

From the flavour of this book you can see that I'm
guilty on both fronts and so when the chance to build our
own home came along I grabbed every piece of eco
nonsense I could get and started reading.

Whilst I have an academic qualification in all things
green I am probably as guilty as most in selling out to some
degree in the name of convenience and making a fast buck.
But that was the past and as you know having waded
through the introduction I turned my back on the money
and started again. Before I stand up and start shaking my
tambourine let's agree a level playing field on what it
means to bring an environmental conscience into a self
build project, starting with a definition.

I suggest the much misunderstood prefix 'Eco' to be
a fitting start. The word Eco derives from the word Ecos
meaning home. Home, in the broader sense of a particular
pile of bricks, means the planet Earth. It's certainly beyond
the scope of this book to solve the world's problems, that
would be the next book! So to make a logical jump it's

about how we build our own new homes, what we use in their construction and what impact our activities have on the planets once we live on them. In terms of home construction the following are of particular relevance :

Materials used in the construction
Energy
Pollution
Water
Reclaim and re-cycling

The British house building industry is as about as traditional and narrow minded as you can get and new ideas and innovations are often frowned upon and viewed with extreme suspicion. Take, for example, the way timber framed houses are viewed by the trade and sadly often by the public. Something that has greater insulation, costs less to produce in energy terms than a burnt lump of clay, and involves a renewable resource has to be worthy of serious consideration. Ask most house builders and nine times out of ten it's block and brick that win the day.

At the design stage I seriously thought about using straw bales in our construction. Barbara Jones of Amazon Nails (what a great name for an all woman construction outfit) sent me a very informative pamphlet about the process along with some references to some aged dwellings in America where the system has been used for decades. Could I get the local authority to even consider the material? No. I then made suggestions for a rammed earth dwelling. Stony silence. Had I not been desperate to get started on getting started (on account of being homeless) I would have fought a little harder. The main point is that viable alternatives to bricks do exist. Often they are cheaper (which is always good news) and have less impact on the earth's resources.

Moving inside the home we should consider what can be used to insulate the walls and roof space. Fibreglass costs more to produce in terms of energy input than a sheep grazing on a Welsh hill. Unfortunately, the sheer glut of the product means that fibreglass is cheaper than lagging your walls with wool. Recycled newspapers make for very efficient insulation and use a freely available source of recycled materials. The downside is the same for any marketable commodity in that it is subject to the market forces of supply and demand and the price can vary wildly. This really is the bottom line for many would be builders and in my experience many eco-friendly materials can cost more than the stockpiled oil industry driven products most likely available from the builders merchants.

Things are thankfully changing and the more people ask for these products the more market forces will come to bear. If your ethics and wallet are up to the challenge try asking your main supplier whether their timber comes from sustainable plantations such as the Forest Stewardship Program (which to their credit has been adopted by my local DIY store).

I tried asking my builders merchants if they could source an environmentally friendly paint. That sent them into a flat spin! That was a couple of years back and I do know that places like B&Q and Homebase now stock eco-friendly paints. Small steps!

In the home there are three main areas where we use energy – heating, cooking and lighting.

Let's start at the source with the boiler. If you have a new home to build and a blank piece of design paper check out the efficiency of the boiler as a priority. There are all manner of clever things going on with boiler designs (e.g. condensing boilers, energy stores, secondary heating systems etc).

Likewise, compare the fuels used and the alternatives. Traditionally, folks will opt for a fossil fuel source, these being the most readily available. Wood fired boilers have come on a long way since the early Aga type heaters and have added aesthetic value, sometimes doubling up as ovens.

With the future supply of fossil fuels under proper suspicion for the first time this would seem to be a good time to look at what is possible to use in conjunction with the traditional fuel source.

Consider supplementing the heating with solar panels. Can the house be aligned to make the most of the sun? We have a south facing garden and a huge roof area. Unfortunately the planners would not permit the roofline we needed to take advantage of this. We did, however, increase the size of the windows, add Pilkington K glazing and build a stack of bricks to act as a passive heating store in the middle of the lounge. This stack is also known as the chimney breast which we deliberately kept within the room rather than tacked on the end where the heat is lost.

As with the cars of the future, I believe the immediate way forward is to have hybrids which use the old (hopefully, dying technologies) alongside the emerging cleaner renewable ones. The other aspect of how we use the energy in the home is one of how the heat gets distributed. I have spoken at length on the virtues of underfloor heating and will only say here that it is my belief that traditional water driven radiators are archaic, inefficient and wasteful of living space!

We do know from studies abroad (in colder climes) that it is possible to design a home so efficient that no top up heat is required. In fact when we started with dreams of a Scandinavian style abode we wanted so much efficiency that the simple process of rolling over in bed would power the fridge for a week !

I once read a book called *The Natural House Book* and was horrified to learn of the amount of pollution most new homes have in them. Often these come from invisible sources such as the solvents used in paints and varnishes. I had not realised what goes into making such widely used materials as MDF board. There are all manner of what the chemical industry calls Volatile Organic Compounds (VOCs) hidden in laminate floorings, carpets, glues and adhesives. Many of these compounds have been found to be carcinogenic. I suggest reading the book and then start looking at what's in the tin! Thankfully, there are many new outlets producing truly eco-friendly products.

A word of warning: ask for sample pots first and give them a try. Many of the paints we used had the durability of chalk. If possible leave a child's grubby mitts on a wall for a week and then try to wipe them off.

Of special note is the Green Shop in Stroud which has an excellent range and great customer service. On a sad note most these paints come from Germany. Why?

With all the rain around in recent winters and the tangible effects of global warming in clear evidence it's maybe hard to promote conscientious water usage. However, I do believe that water will become a more precious resource in the future. If nothing else most of us are now on water meters. Furthermore, my sewage bill is directly linked to the amount of water we consume so there's the incentive. Water in the home can roughly be grouped as clear (or drinking water) and waste water. Waste water can then be divided into the stuff that goes down the wc and the stuff we chuck down the bath the sink etc, the latter is known as grey water.

Unless you have a well (and the license to use it) drinking water is a given. It's sterilised at source and comes in pipes. The other stuff, however, we can do something about.

I suspect most people wouldn't relish the idea of the sewage making its way down a reed bed. But it's an option and a very eco-friendly one at that. Grey water can be re-used in conjunction with rainwater harvesting and a suitable system. This saves the water authorities the trouble of using strong chemicals and sending it back to you at cost!

Much has been written in the DIY and self build media regarding the use of reclaimed materials. It is a strange irony that because of the popularity of all the DIY programs on TV the price of reclaimed materials has increased significantly. From an eco point of view though, reusing building materials makes a lot of sense. There are several reclamation yards around the country, some of which even specialise in reject materials such as insulation materials.

Adding it all up it comes down to a compromise between an ethical decision to minimise the impact on the environment and one of cost. In my experience, eco-friendly materials often cost more mostly due to the prevailing market forces. If more people start asking questions like why builder merchants do not generally cater for the green buyer alongside what exactly makes up a particular product then they will become more readily available. What is encouraging is the plethora of new technologies and innovations that are coming onto the market and the greater choice we now have. In an ideal world we will have homes that are aerodynamic, that blend in with their surroundings and that have a sense of integration rather than dominance of the local environment. When we built we could not afford a home with all the green aspects we desired. The compromise we came to was a pragmatic one, based on an examination of each individual aspect of the build.

For us these were: energy efficiency (including insulation), design (e.g. passive solar) and low risk internal materials. Longer term – if funding ever permits – we plan to install solar panels and maybe look at wind power to harness the monsoon that whips around the garden.

In summary I think it's easy to have an idealistic view of turning our homes into self sufficient low impact dwellings. Nonetheless, I have always aspired for just that. In reality we have to look at what we can do within the constraints of the planners and our budgets as well as optimising the opportunities we have inherent on site. One example of which is the use of wind power and the physical solar aspect within the primary design. At this time there is a massive build program going on in the country. More than ever we have a chance to rethink the way things are done.

My belief is that the single greatest obstacle to radical environmentally sensitive design is blinkered and closed thinking on the part of the local and national authorities. Why, for example, is it so difficult for individual self builders to tender for smaller plots of land?

With the momentum of initiatives such as Local Agenda 21 still in full stride why is this government backed initiative not receiving more support locally?

After all, proportionally, the land owners would make more money breaking up the plots into smaller pieces. As I say in the early chapters, maybe the thought of individual expression in our home design ruins a "let's all look the same way approach". If and when I build again I plan to jump on the bandwagon of getting a syndicate together to compete with the spec builders, possibly using the internet as a tool of communication.

Do the research, make up your own mind and may the force be with you!

Chapter 11

The final frontier – to blindly go

Well done! You've made it to the final chapter and you cannot wait to get onto the list of half a dozen land agencies. Then my work is done. Before I go, I thought I would cap it all off by bringing the story up to date followed by some closing thoughts on the highs and lows of it all. The dateline is now June 2001 and whilst it is true that we are still picking at things, it's all done. Well that's my definition. Technically we received the completion certificate after 18 months, but seeing as that mostly reflects on your ability to do the functional and statutory aspects of the build, that could mean anything. What it really means is that it took six months to move into the shell, a further 12 months to get all the flooring and decorative items in place, and another six months to unpack all our belongings. At about three years on we are now tackling the garden, starting with a raised decking. Another film crew turned up recently and this time we will be on the TV "early in 2002". I didn't even have to quote from Macbeth to get the part.

Mandy and I are still married but the balance of power has shifted to the extent that I wear a tighter rein and I am not allowed near any builders merchants with any loose change in my pockets. Any suggestions of doing this again are met with conditions to rival those of Mr Y. Firstly, there will be a home, a proper home, with a roof, doors and hot running water, all of which would be hired during the build. Hands off rather than hands on, this time I would only project manage. All of this is a big if. I think the possibility does exist but I think it will be a long time before the idea re-emerges. Okay, so maybe in about five years time if we have the inkling, energy or money, perhaps we'll do it again. By then eco-friendly products will be a lot cheaper and land plots much easier to come by. No, I don't think the latter will be true. I do think that what are termed brown field sites will come to the fore. These are the pieces of land that had a past use. For example, old petrol stations or industrial areas. Whatever it is, my aim would be to build a structure that takes advantage of the physical environment it finds itself in.

For example, with the best technology in the world a certain amount of heat loss will occur through the external fabric so why not locate the structure semi in the ground itself. The soil then acts as both an insulator and as a potential heat sink. A southern aspect and plenty of glass to capture solar heat would be next on the design brief followed by some nifty electronic management systems to recover lost heat. To top it off a sauna located squarely in the centre of the dwelling. This then acts as both a source of heat and a source of fun.

Well a boy can dream can't he? Thinking about it, it would look like that place that the Teletubbies live in. I wonder if that was a self build? Ahh hoo!!

Looking back I am glad we did have a go. It was an itch I had for a long time and the home we have is unique and reflects both our personalities and lifestyle. It has also afforded me a chance to change careers since on the back of this build I launched (or floated) a writing career complete with exposure on TV. I think maybe Handy Andy is safe for the moment but now I'm in the garden who knows? First off, I would have to learn to say "Fantastic" a lot, very loudly. But I do have the hair!

Back to the immediate future, we have just under two thirds of an acre of garden to develop. The overall mandate for the garden space is a combination of sustainable living and sprog friendly utility, starting with a raised deck and a "curved at the edges" fantasy lawn area for junior. Well that was the plan at the point of going to print. If nothing else the current popular TV coverage of all things "home design" have woken people up to the possibilities of doing something different. None more so than this little effort. We further plan to divide the garden

144

into three main areas. The first as described focusing on entertaining and child coralling. The second a wildlife, relaxation area complete with pond (all made child safe of course). The real jewel in the crown will be (over a few years development) the mini forest garden at the far end. This will be loosely based around Robert Hart's definitive "Forest Garden" philosophy. This is a branch of permaculture (i.e. all year food production) that bases garden design on the shape and interactions found within a woodland ecosystem. The aim is to work with nature rather than controlling it. So cultivation is kept to a minimum with groups of plants that work together in the wild being deployed in a layered approach (i.e. trees down to root crops). It's beyond the scope of this book to go into much detail, but if I have whetted your appetites get the book, it's inspiring.

From the text you will have seen that self build is a bit of a roller coaster at times. The highs come with the realisation that the land is yours at last. Things can get moving as it is only now that vendors will take you seriously. So you ride down the next hill to the planning application and all the frustration of bureaucracy at its worse. But you climb back on with the advent of planning permission and the first stages of the build.

Our highs were seeing the frame rise Phoenix-like out of the ashes of our lives at that point in time. This was followed by special buzzes (not literally) when the electrical and plumbing systems kicked into life. The lowest point had four legs and whiskers, rats. We've not seen them for a while. Maybe the Uzi in the loft gave them a hint.

Mandy has her own take on the above, but rats are in there at number one by common agreement. At the end of it all I applaud and respected her staying power. I also smiled a lot when she fought off the workmen at 5am to get first dibs in the portaloo.

Maybe the toughest thing was living with an eccentric hippy determined to change the world from his back garden. Whilst my obsession to do everything may need professional help in time, we did have a few laughs from it. At one point I had a number of friends convinced that we dug raw clay from the garden, built a primitive kiln and fired our own bricks. Not that the thought hasn't occurred to me, you understand.

It's true to say that we thoroughly enjoyed meeting and working with 99% of our tradesmen. From Ron who shaved his head and his eyebrows, before being plagued with sweat running into his eyes, to Sinbad living at the other extreme of life. To each a toast and fond memory. I had originally toyed with the notion of a section named "the good, the bad and the indifferent". Certainly one local builders merchants fell under the latter category. Instead, I offer this advice: When you next walk into a builders merchants asking for help, take stock of how comfortable the experience was for you. A good reception would involve some degree of conversation aimed at getting to the bottom of what it is you actually need, without you feeling like the village idiot.

One chap, well known in these parts, would look me up and down, clear his throat and enquire out loud as to exactly the branch of trade I belonged. My first reply was "me, I'm the public, the customer, you know that branch of the trade that is always right and pays your salary". This I followed up with a letter to the regional director, followed by a relocation of my account to another company. In this, trust your instincts. There are plenty of ponds out there for us minnows.

Overall I think the hardest part of self build is this feeling of lost time whilst the rest of the world gets on with its life. We must have issued hundreds of I owe you's (IOU's) for returned dinner parties many of which perhaps we never will redeem. Hobbies by necessity got sidelined along with access to all our favourite toys.

However, whilst self build can be all consuming it is important to keep something back for yourself. Towards the end of the build I took up an evening class which had absolutely nothing to do with building. Not a brick nor scaffold plank in sight, more delusion, pure joy!

The final frontier – to blindly go

I think the process of self building has also made us realise that we are able to achieve much more in life than we might originally have thought, and at the end of it all, even the sceptics amongst our friends and family now walk around open mouthed and enthusiastic. We have a culture in this country of mentally under achieving before we even begin to look at the possibilities and I think this probably represents the largest single obstacle to having a go. Notwithstanding the financial obstacles, I believe that building your own home is within the reach of most people.

To balance that, you need to look at how this would fit in with your current lifestyle. Without question we put our lives on hold for the best part of four years. The first year and a bit was just spent looking around and researching.

So are we wiser, richer, poorer, sad, happy or indifferent at close of the day? Certainly wiser. Richer in our lifestyle definitely. Financially the expenditure to market value ratio is estimated at about one to three. Poorer, no way. Happier, yes. Indifference; I can't make my mind up about! The biggest lesson of all comes in three parts. Research, plan and then believe in what you're doing. Above all else enjoy the job.

So when it's all totted up what is the balance of opinion on the ups and downs of our particular project. Glad we did it? You betcha. We have a dream home that we could not afford to buy on the open market, enough space to indulge our hobbies, and enough memories to fill this book. Most importantly we now have the home we wanted which is as quirky and eccentric as the people and wildlife that built it, all of us, two legs and four!

I wish you all the very best luck. More than this I hope that some of you do feel inspired enough to have a go for yourselves, even if I don't get a holiday out of the book sales!

APPENDIX A – Plan of works
This is a guide rather than a plan that fits every build

Pre construction activities

Research construction options
Design initial build model
Construct financial model around build model
Initiate land search options
Initiate fund-raising activities
Finalise design brief
Obtain planning permission
Finalise funding
Decide on accommodation during build
Initiate legal and warranty cover during build
Site preparation
Soil survey
Foundation design if applicable

Construction

Clear oversite
Setting out
Excavate foundations
Drains and services
Muckaway
Concrete into foundation
Blockwork
Construct block and beam floor
Timber frame erection
Doors and windows
Chimney construction
Roofing
External cladding
First fix commences
Second fix commences
Decoration
External works and landscaping
Completion certificate (could be anytime after second fix starts)

Ancillary activities

Project management
Budgeting
Materials and delivery
Statutory (building control) and warranty inspections
Complete VAT return
Receive VAT refund and celebrate!

APPENDIX B – Glossary of Terms

Back Syphoning
Process whereby a pressure differential between the supply and a domestic reservoir means that soiled water can be sucked back into the national supply system.

Block & Beam
Type of pre-cast flooring structure. Beams cross the over-site with in-fill blocks completing the structure.

Blockwork
Phase of foundation construction when large blocks are used to build on the virgin trench foundation.

Caulking back
Term used in drylining/artexing whereby the joints of the plaster-board are given a final coat prior to the last coat.

CLS Canadian Lumber Stock
Timber commonly used in timber framed construction due to its superior load bearing qualities.

DPC – Damp Proof Course
Plastic sheeting used to prevent moisture moving between material.

DPM – Damp Proof Membrane
Drylining process of tacking plasterboard to studwork, finished with either all-over plastering or seamed and taped edges (plus finish).

Dual (Double) Pole
Electrical switch which isolates both the live and neutral terminals.

ECA
Electrical Contractors Association.

Facing Bricks
Particular specification of bricks used in external cladding.

FCU – Fused Connection Unit
A particular type of electrical connection which has a fuse built in.

Flashing
Lead-work used to seal and bridge areas between brickwork and for example roofing materials.

Flue
As in chimney.

Footings
Part of a particular type of foundation whereby trenches are dug and filled with readymix cement.

Heave
Expansion of surrounding soil/rock in response to local conditions. E.g. clay expands when it gets wet.

IEE
Institution of Electrical Engineers.

JCB
Large digging, multi-purpose tractor.

Lathe (faced)
Metal meshwork used in the application of external rendering.

Manifold
As in underfloor heating – specialist pipework used in the control of the flow and return aspects of the system.

MCB – Minature Circuit Breaker
Modern equivalent of the fuse.

MFC
Melamine Faced Chipboard.
Nogging
Wooden support timberwork which sits behind the plasterboard.
Obi Wan Kenobi
Fictional mystical warrior from *Star Wars*, akin to eastern guru.
Pattress
Boxes which are screwed to the wall or nogging prior to the final fixture being mounted (e.g. plug sockets).
Picard, Captain Jean Luc
Fictional character in TV's Star Trek.
Predictor
Home pregnancy testing kit!
Purlins
Decorative feature used in roof construction.
RC35
A particular mix of concrete.
RCD – Residual Current Detector
Part of the protective circuitry used in the modern fusebox or consumer unit.
Regs. or Regulations
(i) Electrical standards maintained by IEE. Also (ii)Regs. – technical drawings produced to satisfy the statutory requirements of the local building control officer.
Screed
A layer of strong mix concrete used on the floor to (in this case) cover the heating elements.
Setting out
Process of determining the exact location of the foundation excavation required.
Slump
A criteria used to determine the consistency or "thickness" of concrete, exemplified by the way a mound of cement finds its own level.
TCT – Tungsten Carbide Tipped
Used on cutting edges of saw, drills etc.
Theodolite
Surveying equipment used in setting out.
Tie Bars
Metal rods placed in wet cement to add strength.
Toetectors
A particular brand of steel toed boot.
Topping Out
The phase of the build when the highest point of the construction is reached, usually on completion of the chimney.
TWE – Twin Wire and Earth
Cabling having sheathed Live and Neutral wires with Earth left bare with cable housing.
Uzi
Type of sub-machine gun of Israeli design – jokingly referred to as a means of controlling vermin!
Vapour Membrane
Plastic sheet attached to the inside of the timber frame to prevent any ingress of moisture.
Wall Ties
Pieces of metal tacked onto the outside of the frame before being bedded into the brickwork course on the outside cladding.

APPENDIX C – BUDGET MODEL
Paid items indicated in **bold**

	Net Cost	VAT	Gross	Subtotal	Returned
WARRANTIES/INSURANCE					
Zurich Registration	50	9	59		
Zurich Warranty	780	0	780		
Insurance(PubLiab,Employ,Contractors)	366	0	366	__1204__	
LEGAL					
Conveyancing	250	44	294		
Land Registration	90	0	90		
Search Fee (Local)	50	0	50		
Search Fee (Water Drainage)	17	0	17		
Search Fee (Common)	6	0	6		
Telegraph Transfer ~1	24	0	24		
Telegraph Transfer ~2	24	0	24		
Land registery search	5	0	5		
Mortgage legal Fees	205	19	223	__732__	
PLANNING PERMISSION					
Preparation of design and plans for DPP	332	58	390		
DPP appplication (South Cambs)	180	0	180	__570__	
BUILDING REGULATIONS					
Preparation and submission	332	58	390		
Statutory Fee	80	14	94		
Site Vists (@52.75 per visit) for 4 visits	180	32	212	__696__	
SITE PREPARATION					
Soil Investigation - Structural Engineer	200	35	235		
Soil Investigation - Structural Engineer	85	15	100		
JCB Hire soil stripping	112	20	132	__466__	
GROUNDWORKS					
Lorry Hire for muck away	735	129	864		147
Concrete	842	147	990		188
Concrete	1076	188	1265		1
Setting Out Pegs	5	1	6		2
Nails	10	2	12		1
Wall Ties	5	1	6		2
Febmix additive	12	2	15		28
Aggregate (Crushed Limestone)	157	28	185		46
Metal Re-inforcement	264	46	310		152
Underground Drainage	868	152	1020		10
Pea Gravel	59	10	69		51
Guttering	290	51	340		51
Trenchblocks	294	51	345		

APPENDIX C – BUDGET MODEL

Item		Item Net Cost	Item VAT	Item Gross	Gross Subtotal	Likely VAT Refund
Regrades Bricks		258	45	303		45
Ballast Mix		36	6	42		
lockwork labour to dpc		985	0	985		
Groundworker Labour		1727	0	1727	8483	
SUSPENDED FLOOR						
Brickwork under Beams & Cuts		40	0	40		
DPC under beams		150	26	176		26.
Block & Beam floor (incl. ventillation)		1425	24	1674		249
Labour		255	0	255		
Crane Hire		140	25	165		
Insulation Material above B&B structure		198	35	233		35
Staples		9	2	11		2
Screed Labour		360	0	360		
Screed Materials		457	80	537	3451	80
SERVICES						
Temporary Portaloo		246	43	289		
Electricity Board Charges		865	0	865		
Electricians Labour to Temp Supply		138	24	163		
Final Inspection (Periodic Insptn Cert)		143	0	143		
Connection Charge temp to permanent	pc	92	16	108		
Fresh Water Temp standpipe connection		1329	8	1329		
OFWAT Refund		(43)	0	(43)		
OFWAT Refund #2		(160)	0	(160)		
Water Pipe to stopcock		23	4	27		
Telephone connection		99	17	116	2837	
FRAME ERECTION						
Scaffolding Hire		1920	0	1920	2828	
	mg	773	15	908		
TIMBER FRAME		14550	0	14550		
Deposit to Medina	mg	1648	0	1648		
Velux Windows		806	0	806		
Paints and Preservatives		92	6	40		6
Internal Doors plus Furniture		200	35	235	17279	36
ROOF						
Materials		1647	288	1936		288
Marley Refund		(278)	(49)	(327)		
Labour		880	0	880	2489	
CARPENTRY						
Second Fix		223	39	262		43
Lead Flashing		75	13	89		13
Sundries		114	20	134		19
Fascia Boards		82	14	96		14
ELECTRICAL						
Meter Cupboard		18	3	21	581	3

APPENDIX C – BUDGET MODEL

	Item Net Cost	Item VAT	Item Gross	Gross Subtotal	Likely VAT Refund
Entry Pipe	2	0	2		0
Goods	935	164	1098		167
SWA Cables tba	33	6	39		6
PLUMBING				1161	
Underfloor Heating System	2709	474	3183		474
NuHeat Optimiser CAD	50	9	59		9
Oil Fired Boiler (incl Flue)	515	90	605		90
Core Drill Hire	7	1	8		
JG Plumbing	917	161	1078		125
Oil tank (incl fire valve)	292	51	343		51
Heated Towell Rail	294	51	345.		51
Sanitaryware Ensuite	871	152	1023		152
Sanitaryware Bathroom	271	47	318		47
Sundries	2230	40	270		40
EXTERNAL CLADDING				7233	
Bricks	2403	421	2824		421
Lintels concrete	82	14	96		14
Sand & Mortar	351	62	413		62
Labour (Brickwork)	1280	0	1280		
Angle Grinder hire	15	0	15		4
Wood Stain (Timber Black)	25	4	29		30
Cladding	171	30	201		
INGLENOOK FIREPLACE				4859	
Engineering Bricks	5	1	6		1
Chimney pot	14	2	16		2
Flue Liners etc..	116	20	136		20
Convector Box	577	101	678		101
Labour	800	0	800		
DRYLINING				1636	
Plasterboard	600	105	705		106
Plasterboard Returned	(17)	(3)	(20)		
Labour	1100	193	1293		
Plaster Coving	79	14	93		14
Gyproc Adhesive	5	1	5		1
Artex Paint for ceiling	27	5	32		5
KITCHEN				2108	
Kitchen	1055	185	1239		143
Mastic Sealants	0	0	0		9
EXTERNAL WORKS				1239	
Garden levelling (Hunts Hire JCB) pc	124	22	146		
Land Drainage	66	11	77		
Fences	190	33	223		11
Fence Labour	245	0	245		35

153

APPENDIX C – BUDGET MODEL

	Item Net Cost	Item VAT	Item Gross	Gross Subtotal	Likely VAT Refund
Paving slabs	110	19	129		
Lorry Hire for muck away(2 loads)	19				
Driveway Labour	160	28	188		
Driveway Materials	640	112	752	2638	133
GARAGE					
Trusses	211	37	248		37
Trusses Labour	100	0	100		
Roofing Labour	190	0	190		
Tiling Materials	150	26	176		26
Lintel	65	11	76		11
Door	300	53	353		35
Foundation	86	15	102		15
RMC	183	32	215		31
Flexcell (33m is 14 lengths @1.26ea)	18	3	21		3
Brickwork labour	850	0	850	2330	
TOTALS	59886	5001	64819	64819	4050
Statutory Fee	80	14	94		
Soil Investigation - Structural Engineer	200	35	235		
Soil Investigation - Structural Engineer	85	15	100		
JCB Hire soil stripping	112	20	132		
NuHeat CAD & Deposit	50	9	59		
Kitchen Sink	84	15	99		
Kitchen Top	77	14	91		
Sanitaryware Bathroom	271	47	318		
Subtotal	959	168	1127		
Balance	(959)	(168)	(1127)		
Options for us to also fund					
Mortgage legal Fees	205	19	224		
Zurich reg & warranty	839	0	839		
Site Vists (@52.75 per visit) for 4 visits	180	32	212		
Water Connection	1329	8	1329		
Electrician Builders Box	138	24	163		
Electric Connection	865	0	865		
Medina Deposit	1648	0	1648		
Subtotal	5204	823	5277		
Balance	(6163)	(251)	(6405)		
Actual Funds left in Fidelity (est.)	0				
Balance			(6405)		
Actual Loan Taken Out	53000				
Balance overdrawn			(59405)		
Actual VAT refund due	5001				
Funds Left to us on completion			64405		